Not Just Black and White

A White Mother's Story of Raising a Black Son in Multiracial America

Anni K. Reinking, Ed.D.

Read the Spirit

For more information and further discussion, visit

NotJustBlackAndWhiteBook.com

Anna R. Renking

The Starfish Story

The Starfish Story, also known as The Star Thrower, originally was a 16-page essay written by natural science writer Loren Eiseley in 1969. The adapted version, seen here, still encompasses the meaning of the original story: You might not be able to change the entire world, but at least you can change a small part of it, for someone.

One day, an old man was walking along a beach that was littered with thousands of starfish that had been washed ashore by the high tide. As he walked, he came upon a young boy who was eagerly throwing the starfish back into the ocean, one by one.

Puzzled, the man looked at the boy and asked what he was doing. Without looking up from his task, the boy simply replied, "I'm saving these starfish, Sir."

The old man chuckled aloud. "Son, there are thousands of starfish and only one of you. What difference can you make?"

The boy picked up a starfish, gently tossed it into the water, and, turning to the man, said, "I made a difference to that one!"

This book is first dedicated to my son, Ahmad. You are my world.

This book is also dedicated to all the individuals in my life who push me, support me, and make me think outside the boxes of race.

Contents

Foreword

By Elisa Di Benedetto

What is race? How do we define identity? How does education affect our life and relationships? Welcome to Anni K. Reinking's world, where even the smallest occurrence of everyday life raises new questions and reflections, involving sociology, anthropology, religion and psychology.

Not Just Black and White is Anni's emotionally and intellectually moving memoir of her life as a white mother raising a black son in multiracial America—but it is so much more than that. While her story is based in the U.S., this is a global story. Entire nations, and communities within them, are changing as millions of people move around our planet.

As a journalist based in Italy, my vocation over many years has taken me to hot spots where the movement of peoples is sparking change and sometimes conflict. I have reported on these challenges. I have worked with countless men and women trying to make new lives in new countries. This is not a distant story for anyone in today's world. Personally, I know family members and neighbors who are grappling with the dramatic changes we are seeing in our diverse communities. It's likely that you, as a reader, can say the same thing.

In September 2018, Pew Research reported that more than 40 million people living in the United States were born in another country making the U.S. the home to more migrants than any other nation in the world. But Anni's story of changing attitudes toward race and ethnicity is global in its impact. In the same report, Pew researchers say that more than 2 million migrants have come to Europe over the past decade across the Mediterranean. Millions of people also are moving across Asia, the Middle East, Africa and South America.

That's why the stimulating insights in Anni's book are so timely. As a journalist, I have circled the globe reporting the big stories about these movements. Wherever I go, I know that the final story I write must be told through the lives of individual men, women and children. That's what connects all of us as people. That's what begins to break down barriers. That's where we begin to realize that we ultimately share far more as humans than any separation we might perceive from color or creed or customs.

For those of us who understand the urgency of sharing these stories, Anni has given us an intimate look at how these changes affect individual families.

As a journalist, I also understand the challenges and the cost of sharing personal stories. Agreeing to open up in this way is daring. So, I was inspired by the way Anni welcomes us into her everyday life as a mother, struggling with prejudice, bias and preconceived notions. As much as she loves her family, she also loves her community and wants America to become a land where multiracial and multicultural differences are embraced.

She doesn't shy away from controversial topics. She raises critical questions about identity, family and race. Then, she shows us how social perceptions of these issues shape our everyday relationships. You'll find funny anecdotes as well as stories of hard times in her family.

That's the transcendent power of this kind of story. As you explore Anni's story, you begin to move with her. Anni takes us around the world in her story: from a little church in an American small town to Kenya; from current America to old, yet contemporary, Europe with its past of colonialism and slavery; from her own childhood to the childhood of her son Ahmad. As you travel with Anni through this narrative, you'll find yourself thinking of your own family, friends and neighbors. Soon, you'll find that her story spins off into your own reflections.

This book is an extraordinary journey towards awareness and learning.

Though her reflections as a woman, a mother, a wife and an educator, Anni invites us to formulate a fresh point of view on a society where visible differences are constantly dictating the narrative, so inextricably entangled in the dichotomies that surround us: *black/white, bad/good, appropriate/inappropriate*. All too often, we find that visible distinctions—skin color, clothing, hair-style, religious symbols—dictate the narrative of our interactions with people we encounter. Allowing ourselves to get involved with Anni's story—sharing her moments of joy and despair—we come away with a new range of responses we can use as we continue to discern differences and relate to the men and women we meet. Along the way, we build our own identities as hospitable, welcoming people.

Ahmad himself represents the priceless treasure of each human life in this world with its unique blend of cultures, experiences and traditions. As you read this book, you will find that the figure of Ahmad is the key for shifting from the black/white paradigm to a black and white model in which diversity is seen as a resource rather than a threat. In a time when millions of people are migrating to other countries, Anni's family, a multiracial family, can be seen as a vital part of the world's future. Anni's story mirrors the fears as well as the opportunities migration is offering to our communities.

Readers who choose to invest the time in reading this book are far less likely to contribute to the problems we all face: intolerance, discrimination and hate speech. That's why I'm taking the time to add my voice to the chorus of those recommending Anni's book. That's why you may want to share this book with a friend who could be changed by the experience of reading Anni's story. As a journalist, I know that's how the world changes for the better—one story at a time that touches us and makes us realize we share far more with our neighbors than might seem to separate us.

That's the final warning I leave with you, as you open this book: In these pages, you will find a powerful message of hope for our world. Once you start, you'll keep turning pages and traveling with Anni. That journey just might change your life, too. You may come away from *Not Just Black and White* with a new understanding of how to treat the men, women and children living all around you.

Read this book—and you may walk away a different person.

ELISA DI BENEDETTO *is Co-managing Director of the International Association of Religion Journalists. She is known around the world for her reporting on migration, religious diversity and peacekeeping. Over the past decade, she has helped to organize global conferences for journalists who specialize in covering religious and cultural diversity—an effort that has taken her to gatherings in South America, Africa, Asia and across Europe. She lives in Italy.*

Preface

By Christine Michel Carter

By the time you read this book, another black man will be killed by the cops.

Strong statement, yes. But the statement matches the severity of the problem: we're living in a racially divided country. Like a hammer, law enforcement has become the claw by which many white Americans remove black people from public settings. Blacks napping in dorm rooms, reading books in cars, shopping for clothes and touring college campuses are examples of the ordinary behaviors that have been deemed worthy of a police report.

This is America.

This has always been my harsh reality, and its intensity was amplified once I became a mother. And as more white women embrace the belief that "love has no color," it's becoming their harsh reality too. Their children—like mine—endure stares while they play innocently in backyards or overhear off-color jokes from older relatives during Memorial Day barbecues. Together our babies live in a place where prejudice does not have an age minimum. Where discriminatory protests can occur in broad daylight, for which only the mistreated suffer deadly consequences.

Thankfully Dr. Anni Reinking and I both have beautiful, free-spirited sons thriving in this world. Which—though they are both still young—shouldn't be mistaken for anything short of a miracle. I believe it's because we not only choose to expose them to America's bias, discrimination and prejudice, but we also guide them via interpreted research and an open heart. Our country is in its darkest hour, and yet, Dr. Anni and I both have our arms stretched to the North Star of unity and inclusion.

I applaud Dr. Anni on the publishing of *Not Just Black and White*. For years I've researched and written for the general public, advocating for equality, uncovering the challenges of black motherhood and revealing the many cultures that reside in our country. However Dr. Anni is doing something I cannot: using stories of her own ignorance in hopes that it will push her colleagues outside of their own comfort boundaries and foster within them a place for growth and reflection.

Enjoy *Not Just Black and White*, and read it with an open mind. However, do not mistake its content for entertainment. Dr. Anni has provided you with a literary catalyst, encouraging the reader through her own memoir to embrace our ever-changing racial society.

CHRISTINE MICHEL CARTER *is a writer and thought leader for marketing to young moms and black consumers. She has been called the "exec inspiring millennial moms," a "mom on the move" and "the voice of millennial moms." She regularly contributes to Forbes, TIME and Entrepreneur and has been featured in The New York Times, Women's Health and EBONY. Carter is also the creator of Mompreneur and Me, the only national inclusive parent and child-friendly networking event. Mompreneur and Me aims to provide like-minded working mothers with opportunities for sponsorship, networking and work-life balance.*

Introduction

By the Rev. Dr. Forrest L. Krummel, Jr.

Anni is my daughter. Ahmad is one of my grandchildren. Their story, like every story, is unique to our family, but it is not unlike the story of an increasing number of families today. Much of her story I did not know until she wrote about it in this book. This story is one of the stories of what America is becoming.

In actuality, this book is really several stories woven together. It is the story of a young woman seeking adventure. It is about discovering the underbelly of adventure. It is about wrong turns and new beginnings. It is the story of a divorced mom, a single working mom, a biological dad and an adopted dad. It is about grandparents, both biological and adopted as well as "alternative grandparents" who were there when needed. All of us wind our way down a new path, a path inhabited by sisters and husbands, cousins and step-sisters, brother-in-laws and uncles as best as we can. Ultimately it is about seeking that illusive land called "Acceptance." There are many stories within my daughter's story, other stories to tell from different perspectives. I fully acknowledge that there will be many more chapters to live before this story draws to a close. But over the years covered in this book, I've been blessed to have a mere bit part in the greater American family story.

My wife and I were the ones she called in the middle of the night and her safe house when she left Chicago. We helped her find her first house in a new city and secure a plumber when needed. We walked with her during the divorce and were there when she married again. We were present during the adoption hearings and celebrated a "new birthday." We walked to school and home with our grandson. We've been there when he's sick and for his school assemblies. We've tried to be there whenever needed for all of our grandchildren. In this aspect, we're like every grandparent, every parent.

We all live in a tumultuous time in America's history. There have been other times in history like this. But this tumult took many of us by surprise. Just when we thought that we were becoming a "color blind" nation after the excitement and promise of 2008, we witness unimagined backlash. We awoke to the reality that change is hard and progress never moves in one direction. Like an encroaching ocean at high tide, there is a steady ebb and flow. Latent passions have been unleashed and prejudices have been given permission to come out of hiding, but they will eventually subside.

I think that every grandparent hopes for a better future, not only for their children, but for their grandchildren and great-grandchildren. It is our most fervent prayer. I had hoped, and still hope, that when my grandchildren have children and grandchildren of their own, that we will be a nation that more fully embraces the vision of America's Declaration of Independence; that we believe all men—and women—are created equal and endowed with certain gifts.

REV. DR. FORREST L. KRUMMEL, JR. *(aka Frosty) is a Presbyterian minister and has been ordained for 38 years. He grew up in Central Illinois and married the Rev. Susan D. Krummel in 1977. They lived in Iowa for 20 years and raised two daughters. They moved back to Central Illinois in 2006, where he is the head minister of First Federated Church. Frosty has six grandchildren who all call him "Pop." As the third generation "Pop" he loves the name and he loves being their grandparent. Frosty is an alumnus of Butler University, Louisville Seminary and McCormick Seminary. When he is not working, he stays active in a multi-generational martial arts workout, plays the bagpipes and is an avid reader.*

1

My Story, Your Story

"Race is not something people can choose to ignore anymore."

Ijeoma Oluo, 2018

"'Being black,' and 'raising black' is different; 'raising black,' I will never truly understand the life or views of a person of color."

A white mother, 2018

*"To the privileged, **equality feels like oppression**."*

Unknown

This is a story of growth, reflection, and the multiple intersections of identities, in a time when identity politics trend on social media and in political discussions. This story is my story, but it also may be your story—perhaps not now, but maybe in coming years, among your children and grandchildren. So, I say to you: Welcome to our world.

I am a 30-something, middle-class, privileged, Christian, heterosexual, anxiety-ridden exercise instructor; a chocolate and peanut butter lover, a social media addict, an early childhood professor, a dedicated educator, a wife, a step-mother, and a mother; I am a daughter, a sister, an auntie, a granddaughter, a niece, a sister-in-law, and a friend; a blunt advice giver, an equity advocate, and a tattooed, world-traveling, white female.

My biological son is black.

My son is much more than most people's first impression; he is much more than the color of his skin. He is a yellow-belt taekwondo student and a bow tie-wearing, competitive swimmer; he is a wrestling lover, a video gamer, an animal fanatic, and a caring, pizza-loving, funny and weird (it's a good thing) brother; he is a son, a grandson, a cousin, a nephew, a friend, and biracial—but to the world, he is a black male.

In the world's eyes, we are not identified by all of our characteristics. What are we, then?

I am white. He is black.

We are so much more than just the outside coating, but our skin color is the first thing that people see when we are out shopping, exploring a museum, getting a bite to eat, going on a walk, or traveling around the world together.

How do we navigate a world that immediately sorts us into these categories—into "white" and "black"? Within the pages of this book, I am sharing a true story for our time—a story that reflects the current reality for multiracial adoptions, marriages, and families. Each year, millions of new families and children become a part of the ever-growing group that shares a multiracial reality. One month after Trump was elected, more than half of the babies born in this country were part of a minority group. Truly, we are in an ever-changing racial society.

I do not mean, in this book, to dismiss race as an issue—quite the contrary, in fact. In 2018, our racial identities are freighted with substantial meaning and potential opportunities, as well as challenges.

While there are parts of this story—my story—that are truly unique to only my life, there are also parts of my story that are relatable by many. My hope is that readers will see their diverse families in the scenes I describe, and that they may even feel that parts of their stories are echoed.

As I selected the scenes to include in this memoir, I was looking especially for moments that raise vital questions and inspire further reflection. Please, ponder these questions on your own or discuss them with friends and family. As a measure of guidance, I will indicate to you, the reader, when a scene is jumping to another part of my life with the words "Scene Jump Cut." Through the scenes described, you may push back against some of my observations—and I welcome that! I urge you to dig more deeply into what is happening today in our country and worldwide. These are stories for you to enjoy, to relate to, and to contemplate. They are meant to serve as a window into your own community and the world.

This is a book for everyone, regardless of your skin color or background.

If you are a white person reading this book, you may learn more than you expect; if you are a black person and/or a person of color, this book is also meant to show you the world from another point of view. Although this book is for everyone—and it is my journey of growth and learning—I want to apologize up-front. This book is not intended to offend anyone, though through my own learning, I know that even if I don't intend to convey an offensive or hurtful perspective, someone may view it as such—and therefore, I apologize up-front and want readers to know that my best intentions are set forward. I am fully aware that as a white person, I will never wholly understand life from the vantage point of a person of color. However, my perspective as a mother who is raising a socially perceived black son has a place in the national conversation—a place somewhere between, within, or bridging the "in" and "out" groups; the "us" and "them"; the "other" and the majority. My story fits in somewhere.

A socially perceived black son: What does that even mean? Throughout my story, I will refer to my son as black, biracial, and a socially perceived black boy and man. Why? Because through my journey, that is what where I am: still figuring out language, still figuring out how we relate to each other, still figuring out how we relate to the world we live in through race. My son is biracial. However, he is being raised by a white mother and father. His skin is caramel-colored and his hair is coarse, and to society, he is a black boy and maturing into a black man. However, my son is also growing up in a setting in which there is minimal interaction with other people of color (not intentionally), and therefore, he must learn the cultural norms of his black heritage through means other than osmosis in his environment. Why is my son seen as black, and other multiracial individuals seen as black? Through my journey I have recognized society identifying my son, and other multiracial individuals, as black is deeply rooted in American history: the one drop rule and the brown bag test. However, my hope is to continue the conversation of remembering and solidifying our knowledge in the history, the tears, the struggles experienced in our nation, while also striving to embrace and accept a different conversation about race. What is that conversation? I am not sure. I am still on my path of learning and growing.

As a wider hope, I wrote this book with the anticipation that people in our nation will continue to learn, reflect, grow, and eventually coalesce on the idea that hatred, -isms, and negativity do not bring our nation together; they rip it apart. When one's perception makes another group, person, or identity invisible or "less than," our nation, communities, and relationships develop an even deeper chasm. A crater grows between "us" and "them." When our visible identities create a society of invisibility or someone's skin color creates a feeling or act of dehumanization, our society is not fulfilling the American ideal of acceptance, freedom, and equality. I understand that my skin color and the skin color of people like me can create a situation in which I am able to be invisible or fade into the crowd. Invisibility is often not a choice for people of color in America, however, which can create fear, judgment, and a feeling of insecurity or inferiority.

As families are becoming more diverse through marriage, adoption, and the outcome of situational experiences, a wider sense of "us" can emerge. Changes in mindset, actions, and conversations can happen; fear will dissipate, and reflection will enable us to create a better tomorrow—a more diverse tomorrow. Change will begin to seep into all parts of our lives. When a wider "us" begins to experience multiformity, transformations will result.

Our nation is divided, and the -isms defined by society are one place in which we find those divided differences. We continue to be separated by race, culture, religion, economics, gender, and sexuality. Within the pages of this book, I undergo the process of identifying my experiences and innermost thoughts. I open up about my own ignorance and the ignorance of our nation, believing that this is a place to begin. I hope that when we recognize our own obliviousness, we create a place for learning, growth, and reflection. Yet in order for ignorance to serve as a stepping stone for a nation of people who understand both one another and how history got us to where we are, we need to acknowledge that, together, we have to open up our minds; vocalize our concerns; and be placed in uncomfortable situations. Being uncomfortable creates avenues for progress.

This story is the story of my progress: how I went from a place of unawareness to accepting my role as a lifelong learning advocate. My journey of learning began when I was very young and continues today, as I discover and reflect on my life: from child to teenager, young adult, mother, professional, and wife. Through this process I have realized that I am raising a son in a world that I do not understand. My son will have extremely different life experiences than I did, and he will have to learn how to navigate in a divided world with *his* identity—as a biracial, male, educated, world traveler; as a Christian with a Muslim name, raised by a white mother and father. At times, his identity will be seen, read, and designed by preconceived notions about who or what he is. In some ways, he will be judged by statistics. We judge books by their cover, just like we judge people by their demographics. While I am aware that, as a white mother, I am probably having fewer conversations about race with my son than a black mother may have with her son, this story is my journey of discovery—of trying to educate and reach out.

My end goal? To be an outspoken advocate for racial equity. Am I there yet? No.

We are all growing and learning in this thing called life. So, here is my journey—told through scenes of my life. I will help guide you through questions, experiences, and reflections, and while reading, I urge readers to openly reflect—and to embrace the racial anxiety and discomfort this book will inevitably elicit.

2

'The Talk' and Black Bodies

"Black bodies and all bodies of color are policed even in radial justice spaces by white 'activists.' This happens in many ways. One way is through 'community norms' or 'ground rules' meant to prioritize the protection of white 'activists'' feelings and egos, by controlling the emotions, expressions, and truth-telling of activists of color."

Paul Gorski, 2018

"But you're not black," the officer interrupted. "Remember, we only kill black people. Yeah, we only kill black people, right?"

Georgia Police Officer, 2017

"For the first time in history, the Bureau of Justice reports that 1 in 3 black male babies born in this country are expected to go to jail or prison."

Bryan Stevenson

While writing this book in the summer of 2018, I posted on my Facebook page—with the "public" viewing option—the question, "What is 'the talk'?" I asked people to respond to me via Messenger. I had many friends and acquaintances reply, but there were three responses that really stuck out to me. Each of these three responders had a different experience in life and a distinct understanding and approach to the term, "the talk."

One friend responded immediately, and said, "The birds and the bees; like the sex talk." This friend is a white mother of a black son.

"Okay, but you have a black son, right?" I responded, trying to help her think more widely about "the talk."

"Yes," she said.

"Is that still 'the talk' when you are thinking about him?" I typed to her.

"Well, 'the talk' when I was growing up—well, we never had 'the talk,' but I knew that it meant sex from my friends who would talk about it. But now, with my son—specifically, a black son—it is about both sex and how to act right when interacting with law enforcement," she typed back.

Beginning to connect with her, I wrote, "Are you ever scared? You know, of him and law enforcement." At this point I was a white mother talking to another white mother, and we were both raising black sons. She has a black husband at home to help her through these conversations, while I do not; I have books, role models, podcasts, and eavesdropping. However, reflecting back on this conversation, I might have been seeking some reassurance—reassurance that our sons would be okay, or reassurance that it was okay to be scared for our black sons.

She took a little longer to respond this time, but finally, she typed back, "I never thought I was until all this news about police shooting people for no reason and all these white women calling the police on black people just living their lives." I felt her pain and frustration through the screen. I felt that way, too.

A little while later, another Facebook friend reached out to me with a response. She was a coworker of mine nearly 10 years ago and is a black, 40-something woman with two grown kids (one girl and one boy). She is a fellow educator, lives in the Los Angeles area, and is open to hearing all sides of racial disputes and discussions. In fact, she often encourages such discussions on her own Facebook page, just to get a wider view of the world.

My former coworker responded via Messenger, also. She typed, "When I hear the term 'the talk,' I think of sex. When I was little my grandmother cocked up her leg and showed me where babies came from when I asked her, when I was 5 years old."

Laughing out loud as I read the words on the computer screen, I typed back, "Haha, oh my gosh. That is hilarious, and probably a little traumatizing." I had tears in my eyes now, from laughing so hard.

Nonchalantly, she responded, "Nah, it helped me with my kids. When they were in middle school I did full studies with exit tickets, videos, and anchor charts about sex."

Amazed at her dedication—but also wanting to probe a little more—I typed, "Wow! Did you ever talk to your kids—especially your son—about interacting with police?"

"Yeah, but a lot of that comes through street smarts also." She doesn't lie. That is true. "Street smarts" is the knowledge you learn while living in communities that see police either as threats, as confidants, or just as themselves.

Finally, one more former colleague messaged me in response to my post. She is a white female with white children, ages 6 and 10, and lives in a Chicago suburb. She is also a fellow educator.

Sitting at my computer, I heard the *bing* and checked my messages. I read, "'The talk' in my family, growing up, was all about puberty and sex."

"Yeah, that is what it was like in my family, also," I typed, as I nodded my head at the computer screen.

I could see she was typing more, so I waited. Eventually, I read her message: "But for my kids, we have more general talks. Instead of 'the talk,' we try to bring in a sensitive discussion of sex and race more regularly. However, we have not had 'the talk' about interacting with law enforcement."

Intrigued, I typed, "Do you think you need to, with your white children?"

Immediately, she responded, "Yes. Just because they're white does not mean they will not have black friends or friends of color. They may interact with police when they are with people who are not white. It is good to teach them; we just have not had that discussion yet."

"Oh, yeah. That makes sense," I typed back. "Thank you!"

A white mother raising a black son; a black mother raising black children; and a white mother raising white children—each perspective was unique in approach and different from the others. None of the perspectives are "right" or "wrong," but together, they are thought-provoking. These viewpoints illustrate that there is not one way; there is not a course; and there is not a helpful guide, other than street smarts, staying alert, and researching.

So my question to you is this: What is the "the talk"? Depending on your own background—specifically, your experience in the world, based on your skin color and gender—the phrase "having the talk" can have a different meaning.

What was "the talk" to me, growing up? "The talk" was about the birds and the bees. "The talk" was about how babies are born. "The talk" was about safe sex; about what Christians believe about pre-marital sex. "The talk" was what we had in health class, in videos shown during the awkward times of puberty, and in giggling conversations with friends. "The talk" was about sex.

What is "the talk" to me now, as a mother of a socially perceived black son? "The talk" now includes the following:

1. "When a police officer pulls you over, keep your hands where he can see them."

2. "When a police officer pulls you over, only talk when spoken to, with 'Yes, ma'am' or 'Yes, sir.'"

3. "When a police officer pulls you over, do not move unless you ask permission. And if they give you permission, tell them what you are doing."

4. "When a police officer pulls you over, you no longer own your body—they do. Do what they tell you to do and always get their badge number. Memorize that badge number."

5. "Be polite and hold your anger because it will be used against you."

What is the difference between "the talk" for a white girl and a black boy? Well, there are many obvious differences. The difference that sticks out most to me is that one is taught in school (sex) and one is not (police encounters). One is fought about in policies (abstinence vs. safe sex) and one is embedded into the fabric of schools, through policies and proce-dures designed to discriminate (i.e. no afros or noisy barrettes); disciplinary policies (i.e. zero tolerance and school-resource officers who can arrest stu-dents); perceptions of "roughhousing;" and the school-to-prison pipeline beginning with suspensions and expulsions of disproportional rates for black boys compared to every other gender/race combination.

Do you know the current statistics of black drivers? Until I started my journey of discovery and reflection, I did not know the following:

1. Black drivers are 23 percent more likely than white drivers to be pulled over.

2. Black drivers are between 1.5 and 5 times more likely to be searched.

3. Black drivers are more likely to be ticketed and arrested on the spot during a stop.

4. As black drivers are stopped more often, black drivers have a 3.5 to 4 times higher probability of being killed by cops.
5. Black drivers are more likely to be abused and dehumanized during stops, if they are not killed or arrested.

As a white girl, teenager, and woman, I have been pulled over by police. Have I ever been harassed? No. Do I ever "sweet talk" the officer with my femininity? Probably. Has being pulled over ever led to my arrest, dehumanization, or the 'owning' of my body by the police officer? No. Actually, in all the times I have been pulled over, I have never once been asked to get out of the car. My passenger was asked to get out one time, though—and that one time was when I was with my ex-husband, Jay, who is a black man with dreadlocks. When I was pulled over, Jay was asked to get out—even though I was driving. Did the police officer unjustly question him? Absolutely. Did the police office put his hands on him? Absolutely. Did I understand what I was witnessing at the time? Hell, no!

Many years later, when I began to do my own research, I came across a Ta-Nehisi Coates book—*Between the World and Me*—and I began to understand what I had witnessed that day many years ago.

Did you know that a black body is owned?
It's true.
Did you know that a black body is not valued?
It's true.
Did you know that a black body can be destroyed without consequences?
It's true.
Did you know that black bodies are killed more for speaking up than are white bodies?
It's true.

While you may not have known these truths, they are evident—in news stories, in personal accounts and in the actions still taking place in communities nationwide. Through my work as a researcher and professor in the fields of early childhood and race in schools, these sorts of questions are often raised—in discussions among predominately white teaching staffs or among a majority-minority student body (a student body that has more minority students [black and brown] as compared to the overall majority population [white] in the country). Questions that push the boundaries of set mindsets are proposed as a way to make educators feel uncomfortable to the point of questioning and change.

These mindsets—which include the concept of owning a black body—are deep-seated in the mentality of American society. Why can white people call the police on black people (black bodies) that are sitting in a Starbucks, selling lemonade, mowing someone's grass, or waiting at the bus stop? Why does Serena Williams get drug-tested more than other tennis players? Arguably, deep in the foundation of American society, black bodies are seen as less than; they are seen as owned; they are seen, by structures and institutions, as something to destroy and devalue.

As author Ijeoma Oluo put it, "Our bodies (black bodies) are curiosities and tools to be inspected and exploited." Black bodies are bodies for police and others to overreact to. If you're black, you probably already knew that; if you are white, this might be the first time you are beginning to comprehend the idea of losing all power of your body to an institution, to a person, and to -isms in our society. Whichever your position, this book is for you. From the black readers who understand race in a second-by-second experience to the white person who believes that racism is obsolete, this book will make you wonder, question, and begin conversations that you may not have had before.

Police brutality, the Black Lives Matter movement, and the demands of NFL players—predominately black—to stand during the national anthem are all deep-seated in the devaluing of a black body.

Do you value black bodies?

I do.

Have you experienced being pulled over for "driving while black?"

I haven't.

Have you experienced being handcuffed or questioned because you are "walking while black?"

I haven't.

Have you experienced "living while black"?

I haven't.

Can you put yourself in the shoes of a black person?

I can't.

Do your genes have the cumulative impact of racial trauma over generations?

Mine don't.

(Note: One doctor, Rachel Yehuda, outlined this last point in her research. She found that serious incidents of trauma (i.e. slavery, the Holocaust, etc.) and post-traumatic stress disorder (PTSD) can be passed down to later generations through family genes. Her research has revealed that when people experience trauma, it changes their genes in a very specific and noticeable way, and so when those people have children—and their genes are passed down to their children—the children also inherit the genes affected by trauma.)

Have you seen people with your skin color shot on the street daily by people (police officers) who are meant to protect citizens?

I haven't.

Have you been followed while in a store because you look "like you might steal something" (because of your skin color)?

I haven't.

This list of questions could go on and on. I would encourage you to reflect on your answers, as I did mine. Whether you answered "yes" or "no" to these questions does not indicate varying levels of "better-ness," but rather life experiences that influence daily interactions, thoughts, perspectives, and, in reality, privilege.

While many people want to believe and hope that racism is null and void in the United States, these few questions demonstrate that it is not.

While some individuals may try to ignore racism or tell people to "get over it," that does not make reality go away. There are hundreds of years' worth of violent racial oppression in our country, demonstrating that pushing it out of sight or out of mind only does harm to our country. Conversely, having the emotional, difficult, and enraging conversations about the generations of racial hurt and trauma is one place to begin.

The reality is that I am not a black boy or a black man. Rather, I am a white female who grew up in a small town in Iowa. I do not have the real-life experience necessary to fully understand the discrimination that accompanies being a black male in America. As a woman in America, I have been controlled, but that is nowhere equivalent to the control and judgment that black men—or people of color—experience when being pulled over by a police officer; when seeing people clutch their purses as they walk toward them; or when they hear the sound of doors locking as they walk down the street. Black people—specifically males (as that is where the majority of my own growth and research lies)—become a "them"; an "other"; and a less valued person, in the eyes of society.

The "other," the "them," and the devalued person in society—that is my son, a socially perceived black male. He is a male who has the skin color of a black person but none of the cultural language, experience, or family knowledge that is passed along as a means to survive in a racist society. When people see him on the street, at a park, or in a museum, they see him as a black boy. People's preconceived notions come into play and they assume he will speak in slang terms, be rougher with the other kids, and may even be in jail by the time he is 18. Now, do I know this for a fact? No. But I have seen the looks and heard the whispers and comments from other parents when my son begins to play with their children. If they got to know my son—or any boy of color, for that matter—I guarantee that their confirmation bias would be challenged.

I am a mother. I have eagle eyes and am hypersensitive to the world around my son. When people see us together, you can see their questions through the expressions on their faces or the words that come out of their mouths. "You don't want to play with him, he is going to be too rough."

Little does that parent or passerby know, my son stopped playing soccer because he didn't like all of the "roughhousing" and the "mean boys" on the field. Little does that parent know, my son is shy, soft-spoken, and hates confrontation. That parent doesn't know that because the implicit bias that "all little black boys are mean and rough" has seeped into their mind and has impacted not only their life and mind, but also the life and mind of their child.

I often wonder about my life as a parent and the lives of other parents. I do not have a close-knit set of friends with children who are socially perceived as black children, so I never know if my experience is unique or common. However, every time Ahmad (my son) begins to interact with new children, my eyes are like that of an eagle, or a hawk. I watch every interaction, try to listen to every comment from afar, and watch how adults interact with him at a new club, practice, or camp. What preconceived notions are they going to (or not going to) act on, in relationship to my son? If my son is left out of a line or they forget to give him a turn, I internally question: Is it because they forgot, or is it because he is black? I also wonder what other parents think when their child comes to them, after the first day of camp or the first day of swim practice, and says, "I met a new friend today. His name is Ahmad." What is the mental picture that that parent creates? What questions do they ask? What are their unspoken biases and thought processes? I want to protect my son from the "mean people"—the prejudiced people, the people who will think of him as "less than"—but I also know that I need to let him grow. I need to let him experience life. I need to provide him with the resources to cope, while also wildly advocating for children like him.

Recently, a multiracial family was stopped at an airport, when a white mother was questioned regarding the legitimacy of her being her biracial son's mother. This news story is all too real to me. I have not been questioned yet, but every time we fly, I wonder if we will be stopped because of the color of his skin or his Muslim-sounding name. Do I always carry his passport with me, even on domestic flights? Absolutely. Do I carry my white stepdaughters' passports with us, even on domestic flights? No. With two white parents and two white girls, who will question us? (Yes, I am aware of my privileged thought process here.) These are the mental processes, the mental dialogue of taking or not taking a passport, that constantly occur in aware, multiracial families.

These mental processes make up just one of the many realizations I have had during my growth process. This journey has just begun and will continue as long as life continues. However, beginning the conversation now—for an ever-changing society with more and more multiracial families—is necessary. This book is needed now.

While my focus, growth, and reflections are based on my son and how I can fight for him in our society, some of my growth is also pseudo-selfish. My son's skin is brown and my skin is white, yet no one who sees me out in society will place me in a group with the other mothers who are raising a black son. I am not welcomed into circles of black mothers—mothers who have a plethora of knowledge to share with me. I am not saying that they have the duty to educate all white mothers raising black children, but can I just sit in the corner and soak up information? Can I hear what I need to be doing for my son?

In 2018, while writing this book, I had one of those "fly on the wall" moments. It occurred during a conference call with other professionals, focused on the anti-biased curriculum—a type of multicultural, all-inclusive curriculum specifically used in early childhood classrooms. (*As a little background note on myself: I am a professor who focuses all of my research on early childhood classrooms and children, along with the anti-biased curriculum, which predominately focuses on helping every student achieve their fullest potential, regardless of their skin color, religion, ZIP code, family dynamics, etc. I have spent years in the field of education as an educator, professor, and researcher, encouraging my colleagues to push their comfort boundaries in relation to race. I assign coursework to my undergraduate and graduate teacher candidates that challenges mindsets and perceptions based on race and gender. While I admit that I am not always politically correct, I am trying, and I constantly push myself—and others around me—to form a more welcoming, inclusive, and accepting society.*)

During this fly-on-the-wall moment, I was one of four professionals on the conference call. Among the others was a middle-aged, black male; a younger (adult), black female; and an older, white woman. During the introductions, we were asked to describe our families. I went first.

I summed up my life in just a few sentences: "I grew up in a small town without much diversity. Both of my parents are ministers, which made our family pseudo-celebrities in our small town. I have one sister, who married her college sweetheart. For college, I went to a Big Ten school and then moved to Chicago, Illinois, living in Kenya for a few months in between. While in Chicago I got pregnant, married, and divorced—in that order—from a black man. I now have a black son whom I am raising with my husband, a white man. We have a blended family, between children from his first marriage and my son from my first marriage."

After I shared, we went around to the other people in the group—people I had not met previously, who were communicating through an online meeting platform. When the black female shared, she stated that she'd just had "the talk" with her son. As soon as I heard that, my ears perked up.

Feeling confident in the moment, I asked, "How old is your son?"

She responded, "He is 8 years old."

"Oh, I just wondered because I have a 9-year-old, and I am in the process of really trying to figure out how to have 'the talk,' when to have 'the talk,' who can help me have 'the talk,' and all of that, because I just don't have the lived experience for it. I can tell him what I have read or heard, but that is different than saying something from personal experience." I faded off, losing my confidence, and stated, "I was just curious. Thank you." I was feeling quite shy at this point.

She responded simply, with "Oh, yeah,"—and somewhat tersely, in my perception. The conference call continued with the next question and discussions. However, I could hardly pay attention. My anxiety shot sky-high. My mind was racing. Was her response—the perceived terse response—just my perception? Was I projecting my anxiety? Or was the reasoning and question behind my statement offensive? I wanted to let her know why I had asked. When I'd made my statement about my son and 'the talk,' maybe she'd begun to make preconceived notions about who I was, based on previous experiences. I hope I did not do something wrong. This is why I feel so uncomfortable asking for help. I don't want people of color to think they are the spokesperson for me, but I need something.

My brain just continued to go in circles.

After my brief brain meltdown, I re-engaged in the conversation and continued in the discussion of anti-biased curriculum in our profession, early childhood education.

This brief encounter will be a common theme in this book. I want to learn; I want to be able to ask questions to other parents or individuals, just as I would ask questions about potty-training, when to start table food, or the best places to buy the shoes our children are going to grow out of in six months. However, race is a touchy, taboo topic. Perceptions are real, and having conversations—or just asking questions—can be perceived in a multitude of ways. How do I find a group of mothers or parents who have had experiences similar to mine? How do I find "my group"?

3

Church-going People

Few Presbyterians find themselves in genuinely multicultural congregations where no single racial-ethnic group makes up 80 percent of the membership. Much of the racial-ethnic diversity, therefore, in the PC(USA) is between congregations rather than within them.

PCUSA.org, 2014

In surveys conducted in 2002 and 2003, fully 91 percent of Gen Y respondents born after 1976 said that multiracial dating is acceptable, compared with 50 percent of the oldest generation (those reaching adulthood during WWII) who expressed this view.

Pew Research Center, 2006

Scene Jump Cut: Circa 2002

Sixteen years ago, in a little church in small-town America:

"You know he is *black*, right?"

The reverend was sitting in his office on a Thursday afternoon when Betty marched into the church. She was carrying an umbrella, which she gently placed just outside the door to the office. Water dripped slowly off the umbrella onto the linoleum, creating a growing puddle. Her heels clicked as she made her way to the secretary's desk. The reverend could see her sit down and begin talking to the secretary, so he continued to work on his sermon for the week. About 15 minutes later, he could sense someone standing behind him. He turned around and there was Betty, at his office door.

"May I come in?" she asked.

"Yes, please. Come sit down. How are you today, Betty?"

Betty sat down in the big, brown chair in the corner of the office, which faced the desk. When Betty sat down, the reverend knew that she was settling in for a long conversation. He was preparing himself for a complaint—or maybe it would be a concern, or perhaps she just wanted to catch up. He was thinking to himself, "Did I miss something this week? Did something go wrong in the church kitchen, and I am just now going to hear about?" He was unsure if this would be a pleasant conversation or a controversial conversation, but either way, he gave Betty his typical jolly smile as she got comfortable.

Betty was a short, sassy, no-nonsense, older white woman in the church who made sure that everything ran smoothly. She was in charge of the kitchen when the kitchen was being used. She was in charge of organizing and making the lunch when there were funerals. She also was in charge of making sure people were doing what they were "supposed" to be doing. Furthermore, she was a mentor to multiple middle school youths, as they went through the youth (confirmation) program. Her personal perception of herself was one of faith and doing the work of the Lord in the church. Although she came across as harsh, everyone knew that her actions, comments, and sometimes side-eye glances all came from a place of love.

After sitting down, the first thing she said to the reverend was, "You know he's *black*, right?"

Betty was from an older generation: a generation before school integration; a generation that saw blacks and whites not conversing, working, or even looking at each other in polite company. She carried with her an older, outdated mindset based on the history and experiences she'd had as a child and young adult. That was her background and mindset when she entered the minister's office that rainy Thursday afternoon, and made that blunt statement.

The reverend had an inkling of what Betty was talking about, but he decided to probe a little deeper into her comment. "What do you mean? Who are you talking about? We have many black people in our community, and they are all more than welcome to attend our church."

Betty huffed, and said, "Well, Reverend, I am talking about *your* daughter. You know that boy she is dating is black, right?"

"Oh, I see," the reverend calmly responded. Although his exterior was calm, he was strategizing on the inside. The first thing he said was, "I understand that you see him as black. But I want to point out to you that his mother is white—she lives right by us. They are a very nice family. And," he continued, "it is interesting that you see him as black since he has a white mother. That is an interesting concept to me, since he is just as much black as he is white. Don't you think that it is an interesting view?"

The reverend was a white, middle-class, educated 40-something that had been the co-head minister at the church for several years. He and his wife, the other minister in the church, raised their two daughters in the community. The reverend grew up as an only child in a central Illinois city. As a child, he had been poor. His parents had limited education and both received their GEDs later in life. The reverend, however, had a strong foundation that allowed him to graduate college not one time, but three times. He received his professional doctorate in his mid-30s. He was able to leave his neighborhood to attend college, to see other parts of the nation, and to widen his view of people. While his parents referred to black people as "the colored" until the day they died, the reverend grew up in a family of acceptance because of the hardships they had faced as a poor, white family. Therefore, on this Thursday afternoon in his office, the reverend was taking his knowledge and experience of living in poverty, educating himself, and stepping into uncomfortable experiences as a way to educate and decrease his personal ignorance to facilitate his conversation with Betty.

The conversation with Betty continued. "But he is *black*," Betty said again, completely ignoring the observation and question the reverend had proposed. "You are not going to let her keep dating him, are you? Do you know what that means? She is dating a black boy. You don't want black grandchildren in your family, do you? Your family would roll over in their graves if they knew you were letting her have blacks in your family. That is disrespectful and I will not allow it. I don't care how nice he or his family is, it is wrong."

The reverend could tell that Betty was getting more and more agitated as she sat in his office, telling him how to raise his daughter. Though the reverend was staying very calm on the exterior, he sternly said, "Betty, I thank you for coming into my office this afternoon. However, I support my daughter in her decision to date him. The color of his skin does not matter to me, her mother, or anyone else in my family. He is a nice young man who makes her happy. But, again, I thank you for voicing your opinion."

At this point, Betty was fully agitated. How could he not agree with her? Again she said, "But Reverend, he's **black**." The reverend appeared unfazed by this attack on his family. Betty's eyes locked with his and, as he explained it later in a retelling to the daughter in question, he could see that Betty finally understood that the conversation was not going to end how she had hoped.

> *"There is neither Jew nor Greek, there is neither slave nor free man, there is neither male nor female; for you are all one in Christ Jesus."*
>
> **Galatians 3:28**

Scene Jump Cut: Circa 2012

This conversation was relayed to me, the daughter in question, several times since it took place. The first time I heard about this conversation was approximately 10 years later—when my mother and I were cleaning out boxes upon boxes of my childhood mementos, during one of my mom's famous, massive "clean out, get rid of everything" sessions. I held up one of my favorite dolls from when I was younger. It was the size of my palm, made of hard plastic, and had black, curly hair and brown skin. On the upper left section of the chest there was a small button—in the shape of a heart—that stuck out. When it was pressed, the doll said, "I love you. I love you," in a small, sweet voice. This doll was my pride and joy, growing up.

That afternoon, sitting in our cold, damp basement, I listened to the story of my father—the reverend—and Betty. Upon hearing this story, I was in shock: I was hurt, but most importantly, I was mad that this was the first time I was hearing about this conversation. Growing up, Betty had been a mentor of mine.

After having the story relayed to me by my mother, I asked a few questions and then kept cleaning—quietly, reflectively. I was reflecting on my relationship with my high school boyfriend, the "black" boy Betty had been referring to in the conversation. We had since lost touch—other than on social media—but I wondered what he thought. I wondered what I had missed during our relationship. I wondered if he had ever been uncomfortable and if I had just had on my white lenses, and hadn't seen it. I have never asked him, though, nor do I think I ever will. Yet I was also reflecting on my time since high school. Many years, many boyfriends, and many life experiences had passed since that time in my life. I asked myself, "Did I miss underlying events due to my life view?"

As I continued to think and go off into my own world, I kept digging to the bottom of each box my mom put in front of me. At the bottom of a box filled with toys, baby dolls, clothes, and all my Pocket Rockers cassettes, I found my one and only American Girl doll. My grandmother had bought her for me many years earlier, and she had also taken the time to make and sew many pieces of clothing for my beloved American Girl doll. The doll I had asked for, as a child—and still have in my basement, as an adult—is the Addy Walker doll. If you don't know much about Addy Walker, she is the American Girl who represents the life of a 9-year-old girl born into slavery just prior to the Civil War. In her line of books, Addy's character escapes to freedom with her mother. As a young girl, I loved reading her story and learning about her life. As a young child, the books really made me think; they made me question; and, as a 9-year-old girl myself, it is through those books that I began my own journey—a journey of discovery and learning that continues today.

I pulled Addy out of the box—the same box she had been in the day I received her from my grandmother. She was in immaculate condition, even though she had been stored for many years in a dark, damp basement. As I pulled her out, I had the realization—out loud, to my mother—"I had a lot of baby dolls that were not white." My mother looked up from the other boxes and the items around the basement that she was sorting. She quietly laughed at my realization, and said, "Yeah, you always wanted the baby doll that was not white. We would take you to the store, let you pick out one baby doll for holidays, and you almost never picked one that looked like you." She continued by saying, "Your dad and I didn't care either way. We did not have a lot of money while we were raising you, so if you wanted a doll that made you happy, we bought it for you when we had money."

"Well, either way, I loved these dolls. They are the memories of my childhood," I said, as my voice drifted off and I started on another box of childhood mementos.

I looked up at my mom and said, "You know what? I remember when I saw my first black person in real life. It is one of my first memories."

"You do?" she said, surprised.

"Yeah, we were living in our old house and one of your friends from seminary came to visit while on his way across the country."

The town I was talking about—the town I grew up in, until I was 9 years old—had a population of 2,500 people. There was one stoplight, one grocery store, one school, a legitimate, brick-lined town square with a park in the middle, and three churches. My dad was the minister of one of the churches—which, in small-town Iowa, meant that our family had the equivalent to celebrity status. We received free bowling games, free movies, and free admittance to high school sporting events. We had the town politicians over for family meals. Furthermore, there was little diversity in this small town. Minority families were in our community for only a few months of the year because the local corn factory hired migrant workers. However, their housing was on the outskirts of town and, other than at school, the migrant workers did not interact with members of the year-round town population.

My mom continued the conversation. "Oh, you must be talking about Patrick. I forgot he visited us at that house. He stuck out for sure when we walked around the square to the pizza place, didn't he?"

"Yeah. From my view, I was so enamored with him. His skin was so pretty and dark. I remember feeling as if I was on cloud nine because he was so 'cool.'"

How did I, as a 4- or 5-year-old girl, embedd in my mindset that black was "cool"? I am a child of the 90s. I was socialized in a way that saw the "cool" of MTV through the speech, clothes, and songs of black artists. I rarely saw people of color in my everyday life, and when I did, I became an even more starry-eyed and intrigued. What were they doing? Why did they look that way? Where did they live (because they definitely didn't live in my town)? To me, as a child—and beyond—learning about people of various religions, races, cultures, and lifestyles was a way I interacted with the world. At a young age I knew that I wanted to know about people, travel, discover the world, and have an open mind.

Reliving my younger life that day, through the boxes of childhood memories, was therapeutic. I was at a point in my life where I was questioning what was next for me. How was I, a 20-something, going to make an impact? I was questioning my place in the world. What does my race say about me? What does my education—and my access to education—say about me? What do my achievements say about me? What does my privilege say about me? What does my access to a healthy diet say about me?

While reliving my childhood that day, I began a long and beneficial process of reflection: reflection on perceptions; reflection on reality; reflection as a way to heal and move forward, from a place of ignorance to a place of lifelong learning, growing, and reality-seeking.

The beginning of that reflection process started when I learned about Betty and her conversation with my father. Betty was offended that I, the minister's white daughter, would date a socially perceived black boy. Until I heard that story, I had repressed the comments and advice received from my friends in high school. My friends and acquaintances, at the time, would ask me, "Don't you think your dad is going to be mad at you?" Or, "My parents don't want me to really hang with you anymore because of who you are dating (referring to my boyfriend's skin color)." In high school, I was ignorant to what those comments meant. I just figured that I would move on and find other friends, which I did. However, that first exposure—losing people based on the skin color of someone associated with me—has long continued, and probably always will. Upon further reflection, I realized that those comments I received in high school were my friends placing their parents' reactions on my situation. While some friends and acquaintances stopped interacting with me, my family was supportive and shared the view my father provided Betty on that rainy Thursday afternoon.

My paternal grandparents—the grandma and grandpa who referred to black people as "colored" in a loving and sincere way—met my boyfriend with warmth. My maternal grandma, who was a widow at the time, was a progressive woman herself. She was the first female principal in a Central Illinois school district and was working in the school district during integration, as an advocate and supporter of allowing equal education for all. In essence, my family was supportive.

My supportive family was (and still is) based in deep religious beliefs that can be summarized by a quote my grandfather wrote on the back of his timecard one night, as he was working the third shift as a bus driver in the 1950s:

*"My variety of Christianity is not used to explain everything.
It accepts and appreciates mystery."*

—Forrest LeDrew Krummel Sr.

Scene Jump Cut: Circa 2011

Ten years after Betty walked into my father's office to "help" him raise his daughter the "right and Christian" way, my dad—still a minister—had another experience with race and church. His first experience had occurred in a small-town church in Iowa; this next experience happened in a large, country club-type church in Illinois. Once again, I was not told this story until years later, but it nonetheless illustrates the questioning, judgment, and backlash my father has experienced because of my life choices.

In the 2010s, my father was the senior minister of a large congregation located in Central Illinois. He had many staff members and was nearing the end of his career. He was making a last impression in the ministry, but was also not stopping. People in the church, both past and present, would describe him as jovial, friendly, welcoming, sometimes absent-minded, and, overall, caring.

I had recently moved to the city where my parents lived because I was 25, had an 18-month-old son, and had just gotten divorced. I needed help with life, child care, and a male figure in my son's life. This was also a time that, in the church where my father was serving as the head minister, was more tumultuous than most due to large financial decisions.

During this time, my father was working hard to support his daughter and grandson. While walking through the hallways on a cold winter day, my father was not whistling his normal, happy tune; he was focused on his next task, so that he could pick up my son on time from the babysitter. He turned the corner to head into his office and a parishioner was in there, waiting to talk to him. This parishioner was a man in the congregation my father trusted, looked to for guidance, and eventually would consider a friend.

"Well, hello. To what do I owe this pleasure?" he said to the man sitting in his office.

"Nothing special. I just wanted to let you know something," the man said. He hesitated, shifting in his seat as he kept his gaze on the floor and twisted his right hand inside of his left.

"OK, shoot," my father said, still upbeat.

The older gentleman started quietly. "Well, I heard two older women talking the other day while they were working in the kitchen. You know who I am talking about," he said, beginning to get a little more confident.

"Yes," my father replied, nodding slightly to encourage the older gentleman to continue.

"Well, they were talking about you and your grandson." At this point, the man made direct eye contact with the reverend.

"What about?"

"I overhead them say that they do not like you having a mixed grandson." And then he quickly said, "Now, I am quoting them here."

"I understand." The reverend nodded, as his face became more serious. The man continued.

"They said, 'I don't think the senior minister of our church should have a mixed grandbaby, and at least if he has to have one, don't have the mixed black baby around him all the time. He doesn't need to show him off.'" The man finished relaying what he had overheard and then added his own comment. "I thought you should know. Now, you know they are older, and might have different mindsets."

"Yes," the reverend said. "I understand. I also understand that I am not going to change what I am doing. He is my grandson. I love him and he will be my shadow on the days that his mother needs my help." His tone did not change, but he said his statement in a matter-of-fact way.

"Yes, I know. I don't want you to do anything different. I just wanted to you to know," the gentleman said, supportively.

"Thank you for letting me know." My father stood up from his desk chair, as had the parishioner, and the two shook hands.

The man walked out of the reverend's office, and nothing changed that day other than the reverend gaining a new bit of knowledge. His actions, his support, and his love for his grandson only grew bigger because he was beginning to experience firsthand (in a way) the discrimination his grandson would experience for the rest of his life. He was sad at that realization, but also hopeful and encouraged to be standing up for someone he loved.

4

My Muzugu Life

"Steve Irwin, Wildlife Master, Is Killed by a Stingray at 44"
The New York Times, Sept. 5, 2006

*"Christian missionaries devote time, energy, and billions of dollars
to helping African children orphaned by the AIDS epidemic. But
sometimes well-meaning efforts can do more harm than good."*
National Public Radio

Scene Jump Cut: August 2006

Kenya: A developing country on the east side of Africa; a country that was a British colony, and that is often associated with government corruption; a nation with a beautiful countryside full of animals that can only be seen at zoos in America. A girl—me, as a 20-year-old—traveled to Kenya after graduating from college one year early.

"The tire. The tire. THE TIRE!" I yelled, clutching the door handle near the front seat, my voice getting more and more frantic.

"What?" Kurt slowly turned his head to look at me. He was sitting in the middle seat of the front bench and did not know what was happening.

"THE TIRE FELL OFF THE MATATU!" I yelled at Kurt. By this point, one hand clutched the door and the other hand was grasping Kurt's thigh.

Grimacing and trying to pry my hand loose, he said, "Oh, you mean like the spare?" His calm voice echoed in the matatu as he stared at me, now with his brow furrowed.

Still gripping both the door and Kurt's left thigh, I replied, "No! The tire that was on the van—it just rolled away! Did you not see it out the window?!" I responded, exasperated and pointing out in front of us.

"Huh, that's weird," Kurt said, seemingly unfazed and, by this point, having given up on trying to pry my nails out of his thigh. I assume he figured it was a losing battle.

"No, Kurt!" I said again, clenching my hand a bit harder to get his attention even more. "We only had three tires for a second. Like, look at this traffic—we could have died! The fourth tire is up there! It rolled away!" I pointed in front of us. About 100 yards away, our tire had stopped rolling and was lying on its side. The matatu driver was walking toward it and using his cell phone, presumably to call someone for help.

Kurt and I were the only two people in the front of the matatu (a van-like taxi) with the driver. We were not buckled in, because most of the matatus did not have functioning seatbelts. We were squeezed in so close that our skin was touching from our ankles to the bottom of our shorts. Our hips were so close that we would have to open the door in order to move around at all. In other words, we were squished together in a foreign, third-world country, and had only known each other for a few weeks. And, our matatu had just been rolling through traffic on three tires.

Kurt looked and me and said, "No, you are joking." He turned around to gaze at the dirt road in front of us. Cars zoomed by, one after another, with seemingly no regard for traffic rules. When Kurt saw what I had been pointing to, his mouth dropped open in shock.

The rest of the people in the matatu, who were all sitting behind us in bench seats, were staring at me, and then at Kurt, and then at the driver, who was now lifting the tire off of the ground at the side of the road.

"Holy shit, you weren't kidding! What is happening?" Kurt finally understood what I had been trying to say.

That was how we, nine young-adult Americans, started one Sunday morning after living in Nairobi, Kenya for nearly two weeks. We were in Nairobi for the initial training and cultural education we'd had before heading to our respective sites for a year of volunteer work. On this specific morning, we were headed to a church, to sing and to meet an American-born missionary minister. We never made it. Instead, we were parked like sitting ducks on the side of the busy road.

We were nine white people with an obviously nervous Kenyan driver, waiting for help to arrive. We were sitting on the side of a dirt road with cars racing by, much like an interstate in the United States. The weather was muggy, the sun was hot, the smell was pungent, and the homesickness was setting in.

A few months earlier: My adventure in Kenya began earlier in the year. I had graduated early from the University of Iowa with my Bachelor of Arts and did not want to be an adult yet, so I had decided to apply for a position as a missionary/volunteer in Kenya, a place I had always desired to visit. After the application process, I gathered with other young Americans who were applying for the opportunity to volunteer somewhere for a year. We gathered in Louisville, Kentucky, to discern and choose a place to live and volunteer.

As the weekend of my discernment progressed, I felt called to work with children in Kenya. For as long as I could remember, Africa had been a place I felt—I knew—I wanted to live one day. And, at the age of 20, my dreams were going to come true.

Fast-forward several months: I graduated from college with my bachelor's degree, both of my father's parents had died within days of each other, and I was prepping to pack up my life to move to the other side of the world. It was a time of major change in my young life.

August 2006: Dozens of American young adults boarded flights heading out of O'Hare International Airport, to travel all over the world for a year. After several flights, I, along with eight other young adult volunteers, arrived in Kenya. We were placed with host families right away, and my family was the Murighs. My Kenyan mother and father were very kind, caring, and welcoming (though since moving back to the States, I have not kept in touch with them). They had one daughter, one son, and a boy that lived with them because he was being sponsored by the family to attend school. He was from the slums of Kenya and needed financial support, along with stability, to attend school. That boy, the "adopted" son, is the only one I truly remember: Giddeon.

Giddeon was full of life, laughter, and a deep desire to learn. This deep, intrinsic desire to learn—which I first saw in Giddeon—was something I encountered and felt throughout my four months in Kenya while interacting with children in a variety of situations. Giddeon taught me numbers in Swahili, how to ask the house worker and gatekeeper for help, and how to navigate my new neighborhood. Yet regardless of how he helped, I was completely out of my element. I was scared, homesick, and getting used to a new and slower way of life.

One day, while my Kenyan mother and father were at work, my Kenyan siblings were at school, and I was left at home with the house worker and gatekeeper, I was sitting in the living room and decided to turn on the television. (*Note: All of the houses had large, locked gates around them, due to robberies and other crimes.*) Sitting in the living room, I decided to see what I could find on TV that was in English. The service was not very good, but I did hear one thing: "Steve Irwin, dead at 44."

What? Steve Irwin, the crocodile hunter? No, there is no way he is dead, I thought. At that sole moment, my world felt as though it was ending. It's not that I was that invested in Steve Irwin, but more so that it was far enough into my Kenyan adventure that I was intensely homesick. Along with the strong feeling of loneliness that I had been experiencing that day, my stomach just dropped—my eyes welled up with tears, and my heart started to pump harder and harder. It had finally hit me. I was in a foreign country, halfway around the world, I was only 20, and I had no one. I was on my own.

I needed to get out of the house. I needed to go somewhere. I needed to get my mind off of myself and my self-pity. I decided to talk to the gatekeeper, to ask how I could go get something to eat, get stamps—anything. He directed me down the road, instructing that I turn right and that the market would be right there, where I could see it. I began walking down the street, kicking the light-brown dirt as I walked along. As I was strolling down the street, somewhat aware of my surroundings, I started getting that crawling feeling on the back of my neck like someone was following me or watching me. I looked up, and everyone was staring at me—not in a rude way, but in a gawking way, like, "Who is this *mzungu* in our neighborhood?" I realized that I was the minority. It was the first time that I had felt this way—my first memory of being a minority—and it has stuck with me since that day. At that moment, when I realized that there was a spotlight shining on me, I became self-conscious; I became scared; I became aware. I realized that I was a white person in a world I did not understand and that I had no context for. I was out of place. What was I doing? I immediately turned around and walked back home as quickly as

I could, without getting any food or stamps. I was too scared, too lonely, too aware, and too out of place to keep going.

When I returned to the house, the gatekeeper asked if I'd had a nice trip, smiled, and opened the gate for me. I smiled back and went directly inside. What was I doing here? I was completely out of my element.

While I was in Kenya, I documented my experiences in a blog so that my family and friends could read the details of my journey. Re-reading that blog has also been a great way for me to reflect on my life, my experiences, and my mindset at that time in my life.

One of my blog entries outlined a letter I had received from Giddeon on the day he left for boarding school:

> *I'm really happy with the kind of love you've shown me as your brother. I never expected this much from you. You have made me to be fully comfortable to this family. It's amazing that I have become one of this family. The way you treated me like your real brother and not like an outcast—a boy from a very poor background—makes me feel that in spite of many obstacles I have encountered to be where I'm [at] there is still hope for me. And now it's back to school time. I have gone but I will miss you a lot. The way we played together, the games we played together like cards, blind man, and PlayStation, I will miss them a lot. I do not want to go. You know how I am feeling, like refusing to go. Remember to put more effort into your studies please. I have told you several times that you are lucky to have someone tell you do your homework, revise and encouraging you to do your best. Your parents are really amazing, wonderful gifts that God gave you. They know what education is and its benefits. For my mum, she never went to school so there is no way she could tell me to do something she never did herself, although to myself I know the benefits. Please pray for me, as I will be doing for you. This is not goodbye because I am not going to die, so I will see you again, don't worry. Annie, thank you for your present, it is the nicest thing I have gotten. You are my sister and I love you. What a wonderful present you gave me; I will live to remember you through them.*

God is with you and good luck. I love you all.

From your bro,

Giddie

I never saw Giddeon again. And to be honest, I cannot remember what I gave him as a present. But, I think about him often.

While with my host family, I experienced my first Kenyan wedding; my first visit to the homeland of my host family, Kikuyu; and my first visit to a Kenyan hospital—an experience I never truly thought I would have. The hospital I visited consisted of many simple, one-story buildings, all connected by dirt paths. It was built by missionaries and run by locals, and assisted by foreign doctors who came during certain parts of the year.

My host mother—whom I called *mama*—took one day off of work to take me to visit her extended family and her homeland, and to visit sick parishioners from her church. Her husband was a minister and, as traditionally occurs in Protestant churches, the wife of the minister is charged with visiting members of the church who are unable to attend. Essentially, she was "calling" on behalf of her husband.

That morning, I dressed in a long skirt and a black T-shirt. I was ready to get out of the house and was anxious to see Kenya. After we ate breakfast and sent the kids off to school, my Kenyan mother said, "Come, we go."

I politely stood up from the table, pushed in my chair, and gave a slight smile to the housekeeper, who was clearing the table. I followed mama out the door. Once the door shut behind me, we walked to her car, which was parked in front of the garage. I got in the passenger seat, she in the driver's seat, and she turned on the stick-shift car. She pulled the car around to the gate, spoke in Swahili to the gatekeeper, and he opened the gate for us. We were off for the day.

We first drove to the grocery store in the larger mall in Nairobi, to get some food and drinks to take to her home village. Once those items were purchased, we began the one-hour drive to her parents' land. This was the first time since arriving that I felt as if I was seeing the "real" Kenya. I saw women walking with buckets of water on their heads. I saw children and men walking around with no shoes. I also saw a dead body on the side of the road.

"Mama, umm, what is that?" I asked, as we inched along in the busy traffic.

"Oh, that—that is one of the slums behind Nairobi and Kikuyu," she said in a nonchalant way, obviously not seeing the dead body on the side of the road.

"Oh, yes. No, but I mean that man. That man who is not moving, at the bottom of the hill there. What is happening?" I was pointing now, and could see that the man was not moving.

Caringly, yet not surprised, she responded, "Oh, dear, he is dead. Rest his soul."

"He's dead? Like, *dead*, dead? Why is he just lying there, with people walking around him?" I tried not to sound shocked, but I was. This was going to be a place for me to learn and I needed to accept that.

"Well, in the slums, they do not want the dead body to smell up everything, and he probably doesn't have any family, so they put his body there. Someone will come along and pick it up."

Traffic was beginning to pick up now and she was concentrating on the road more than the conversation. But I was still thinking about that man. I could not wrap my mind around the concept that a dead person was just lying on the side of the road, for someone with a truck to eventually come and get. This was normal? It was normal for the slum.

I did not respond to Mama's last statement. I just sat in the passenger seat, thinking and looking out the window.

Eventually, we arrived at Mama's friend's house. We were greeted and provided tea and cookies. They spoke for a while in their native language. I smiled every now and then and listened, but understood nothing. Finally, my mama stood up and motioned for me to go outside. I complied. We all hugged each other, smiled, and said our goodbyes. We were off again.

Pulling away from her friend's house, I asked Mama, "Where are we going now?"

"To the hospital. They told me about someone who is there that I want to visit," she responded.

Silently, we rode down the bumpy dirt roads in her stick-shift Toyota until we stopped in front of three or four mud buildings.

"We are here," Mama said.

"Okay." I unbuckled my seatbelt, but buckled my head into this situation. We were at a Kenyan hospital in a remote village. What was I going to see?

I followed Mama around to various rooms, met doctors, and visited with patients, all while saying only a few words and understanding only a few words in response. However, when we were about to leave, the doctor asked Mama and I to visit with one last patient. She was in her early 20s, and was very sick. We walked into her room, and I was nervous—while I had been in hospitals and nursing homes before, this was different. This made the hair on my neck stand up.

"Pray for me," the patient whispered, in English. Mama began to pray, but the doctor stopped her. In Swahili, he essentially said, "No, the white woman prays." Mama turned to me and said, "She would like you to pray for her."

My brain was saying **Ahhhh, *what?*** but my outer body was calm and collected. I agreed. I bowed my head and began to pray. I can't remember now what I said, but I know it was short.

After the prayer, we said our goodbyes and walked out of the room with the doctor. The doctor and Mama said goodbye in Swahili and I smiled, following Mama back to the car. Adrenaline was still pumping through my body. I had been put on the spot. Had I done it right? What was wrong with the girl? What was God asking me to do in this place?

Before we got to the car, Mama turned to me and said, "She had never seen a white person before. She knows that white people are good and wanted you to pray for her because maybe your prayer will be answered." With that, she turned and kept walking to the car. She got in on her side and waited for me to open the door and sit in the passenger seat.

I walked behind Mama, slowly, after hearing that. My brain was racing again—something that would happen often in Kenya. I wanted to appear composed on the outside, but my insides were experiencing upheavals. The first white person she had seen? I am good, so my prayers are answered? What? Holy cow, I thought race would be different here. What did I get myself into? I questioned all of these things.

The day continued. We visited more friends, with me sitting and not understanding most of what was being said. By the end of the day I was tired and ready to lie down. We arrived back to the house around dinner-time; the housekeeper had already prepared food, which was sitting on the table when we opened the door. Everyone in the family was sitting at the table and turned to look at us as we entered.

"Oh, good, you are home," Baba said. "We now can eat."

After spending several days with the Murighs, I was reunited with the other American young adults who had traveled to Kenya. We all had stories to share and didn't seem to have enough time or breath to com-municate it all.

After our home stays, we were transferred to a monastery for the remainder of the month, for training sessions that would be completed before we headed out to our respective sites. The monastery was in Lim-uru, Kenya. The monks, along with the men studying to be monks, were welcoming, generous, and fun. While living in the monastery, many events occurred—including my 21st birthday.

On the day of my birthday, I was awoken to the playing of *Happy Birthday* on a guitar and the other American young adults singing to me. My parents had packed 21 small, wrapped items in my suitcase for me to open on my birthday, which I promptly did. We had a day full of learning, but once we were finished with our daily lessons (which included learning Swahili and Kenyan history) we returned to the monastery.

I had been talking with the monks about my birthday for a couple days leading up to it. They always seemed confused by the stories that we, the Americans, would tell them about our big, American celebrations. How-ever, after moving to Mombasa and living with orphans, I began to gain a different perspective. In an excerpt from my blog, I wrote:

> *Most people in the States take birthdays as a big celebration, especially the "big birthdays" such as 14 (in Iowa), 16, 18, and 21. However, after experiencing our first birthday in our house (similar to a dorm in the orphanage) I realize that they (Kenyans and/or orphaned children) take birthdays completely differently. I have concluded they do this for several reasons.*

> *Some of these children have never had a real party or celebration for their birthday.*

Some may not know their birthday because of lost paperwork or the circumstances surrounding their birth. Some of the orphans I live with just pick a day as their birthday because they do not really know their "real" birthday date. One boy who celebrated his birthday with us forgot it was his birthday because it was just assigned to him. He did not know how old he was "supposed" to be turning because he had just received an age assessment, which are also just a rough guess.

Some of the children do not have birthdays because of lost paperwork or the inability to get an age assessment in a timely manner. Why would a child want to celebrate someone else's birthday if they do not know their date of birth or get a special celebration?

Although the monks may not have fully grasped the idea of large celebrations and birthdays, they did understand my homesickness, so they decided to organize a party for me—a dance party around a campfire! (I love dancing, and campfires bring back so many great childhood memories.)

When we returned from our studies, the monks led us down a path to a clearing in the forest. They had set up a boombox and already had a fire going. When we arrived at the spot, everyone yelled, "Happy birthday!" I smiled my biggest smile and gave each and every person a hug. Turning 21 in a different country was going to be hard, I thought, since Americans place the age of 21 on a pedestal of birthdays. While mine might not have been traditional, it definitely was one to remember. We danced with the monks until late into the night. When we were all tired, we headed to bed because we all had big days ahead of us.

After several weeks in Nairobi and the surrounding areas, it was time to travel to our places of work—basically, where we would be volunteering. My assignment was to live and work with orphaned girls and street boys in Mombasa, Kenya (a coastal community on the Indian Ocean). The children I worked with were seen by society as "thrown-away" children, or "garbage" children. They were the children whom both natives and tourists would pass without even bothering to make eye contact.

The street boys I primarily worked with had hard lives. They lived on the streets, mostly from the hardship of losing a parent or being forced out of their house because it was too expensive to have children. In order to cope with life, many of the street boys would sniff shoe glue to get through the day. They would also sniff the glue in order to be high enough that hunger was not an issue. The glue would suppress their need for food, which was a scarce commodity in their lives.

While the girls were provided an orphanage to stay in during the night, the boys were only provided services (meals and a safe place) during the day. At night, they would be left to fend for themselves, which truly created a sense of family among the boys. In the morning, when the boys would arrive at the center, they would get their staple meal: rice and beans.

Seeing the boys every day, the other volunteers and I created caring relationships with them. We wanted to know about their nighttime lives, too, and so one night, we left with the boys at sundown. We wanted to experience their nightly routines. The boys had been asking us to join them for weeks, so we finally found a night when they could show us their "night homes."

It was amazing to see how excited the boys were to show us how they scavenged for cardboard boxes every night, behind the restaurants and stores. They were able to build a shelter—a sturdy shelter, for the night—with just a few boxes. But they also told us about the police; the getting woken up and yelled at to move. They relayed to us the instability, but also the ingenuity, in finding a place where the police could not see them. Once their structures were set up, one of the volunteers said, "I love your skylight," as he motioned up to the night sky. We all smiled, and with that, we headed off before it got too dangerous for us to be out.

While walking to catch the matatus back to the compounds where we were staying, one of us said, "I feel badly, but I know this is their life." We all continued to walk quietly for a few more steps; our silence was a way of agreeing with that statement. Then one more person spoke up, before we got into our matatus: "We just always have a way out, a way to get more food or shelter, and they don't." With that, we solemnly got into our respective rides or walked further down to catch the next matatu.

That night—along with all of my experiences with the boys—I learned a sense of community, a true desire to learn, a love of life, and the meaning of sharing and giving when there is nothing to give.

This sense of giving was vibrantly illustrated in another experience I had with the street boys. The boys I worked with in Mombasa did not attend school and lived on the streets most days, due to economic issues in the country at the time—but you can bet that every day, they made attempts to help the least, the last, and the lost. About two or three months into my stay, I met a little boy. He was about 7 or 8 years old, and was brought to the orphanage by a group of young men—the young men who, daily, attempted to help the least of these.

The older boys arrived at the center surrounding the small 7-year-old, who was walking with his shoulders bent over and tears streaming down his face. At first, the center director did not know what to say or do. He calmly walked up to the group of boys and said something in Swahili. They responded, and the director—a Kenyan man who had grown up on the streets—immediately put his arm around the young boy and guided him to the open-air kitchen to get some of the rice and beans that were always ready for the boys throughout the day.

After the director led the little boy to the kitchen and got him settled with a plate of food, he walked back to the group of *mzungus* who, at this point, were just standing there, gawking at what was happening.

"His mother was killed this morning," the director said to us in a hushed, solemn voice.

"Excuse me?" one of the volunteers from Belgium was wondering if there was a language barrier to her understanding.

"Yes, his mother was killed this morning by a car. He will need extra support today." And with that the director walked away, leaving the group of *mzungus* to process what was happening.

As the day went on, the street boys who brought in the little boy told us the story while we all sat in the main room of the compound:

Earlier in the morning, the young boy and his mother were on the street, begging in front of a large church in downtown Mombasa that sat on the corner of two busy streets. While begging, she was hit and killed by a car that lost control. The boy was sitting behind her, and was protected from the impact, so he survived. When the street boys saw the accident, they knew that they had to jump into action. They knew that the little boy would be ignored and left by the emergency crew, so they stepped in.

The street boys walked up to him, told him to come with them, and walked directly to the Christian center, where they knew the caring adults would help him and provide him support—the same type of support they had been receiving from the center for years. The young boy was adopted into the street family the moment the accident happened. The love of Christ was shown to him through the actions of the older boys, the actions of the center workers, and the prayers that were said over him multiple times a day.

It is astounding to think that all in one day the little boy witnessed his mother's death, was adopted by the street boys, and was given a place to call home because of those who helped the least of these. The street boys saw what he needed and knew that he was in need. Amazingly, the street boys were never stopped by passersby as they rescued the little boy. European tourists, downtown workers, other people on the street—no one saw this boy as a child who needed help, except for the street boys. They understood that regardless of race, religion, background, or money, helping the least, the last, and the lost was the most important thing. The boys' actions and words changed my life in that moment.

Scene Jump Cut: September 2006
Mombasa, Kenya

One morning, I found myself walking through brown puddles that were running down the sides of the street, giving off a stench I couldn't quite decipher. I was hoping that I did not have any cuts on my feet, because there were always waterborne diseases traveling in the water on the streets and I was in sandals. That morning, I was walking to a funeral—the funeral of a young boy, Steven. This young boy was orphaned as a child and had found the Christian day center as a home. He had the friendliest smile you would ever see.

Steven had gone down to the docks with other street boys a few mornings earlier, to go for a swim. This was a weekly event for the street boys, as they did not attend school and had the desire to find events to fill their day. That morning, the boys who went down to the docks all jumped in, swam around, laughed, got out, jumped in again, and had a fun morning. Before they were about to leave, Steven wanted to do one last trick. He told all the boys to watch as he dove into the water. After he jumped in, the boys waited and waited—but Steven never came back up. He was seen as a "garbage child" in the eyes of locals, and no one tried to save him because they did not know what took him under. They assumed it was a shark. His body never was found.

While walking to his funeral, I recalled the first time I had met Steven. He was part of the greeting crew, when we arrived in Mombasa from Nairobi. When I got off the train that first morning, he greeted me with a hug, a smile, and a friendly hand to help carry my luggage. That morning, he greeted me with the warmth of family. We were family. On the bus ride to the orphanage for girls, where I would be living, we talked about his life, his joy for life, and about all of the things he was going to show me in the city. He loved his city, even if his city sometimes did not love him. Talking, laughing, smiling, singing—I just enjoyed his company on that first ride to the orphanage, I never could have imagined that in just two short weeks, I would be saying goodbye to him forever.

When I arrived, the other orphanage workers were there, as were his brothers and sisters at the orphanage and other missionaries who had known him for only a few short weeks and months. Steven was being recognized, memorialized, and remembered. During his life, he was seen as a "lost boy"; tourists often passed him on the streets. He was often too high on glue to make it to every meal that we provided to the street boys, but he was surviving in the world—*his* world. He came to know God through the people at the orphanage, and he knew that God was with him through his life and would be with him in death. As was evident in our first meeting, Steven showed love to others and never met a stranger. He felt as if everyone was part of his family—a family he'd never truly had outside the walls of the orphanage.

Scene Jump Cut: August 2006
Nakumatt, Nairobi, Kenya

I not only learned from the children I worked with but was also very aware of my surroundings, and made sure to learn something from every situation. The biggest moment of learning—outside of my experiences with the children—culminated in the idea that "white is good." Naively, I assumed that I would be a minority (and seen as a minority) while living in Kenya. Overall, my perception was that I was wrong, and I can pinpoint specific events that proved such, one being my realization while walking down the neighborhood streets of my Kenyan family.

Another event happened while I was walking around Nakumatt with my American counterparts, back in Nairobi. Nakumatt was the local grocery store. While wandering around, I knew I had to get certain things I needed—most importantly some Cadbury chocolate (deliciousness), and sunscreen, as mine was already gone. I found the chocolate easily enough, but I could not find the sunscreen. I was walking around, looking for similar items. Maybe it is by the beach towels? It was not there. Maybe it is by the medicine? It was not there. Then I spotted the bottles of sunscreen.

As I walked closer, I realized that the bottles I thought were sunscreen were not. In big, bold letters, I read the words: *lightening cream*. Confused, I turned to one of my fellow travelers and said, "What do you think this is? Do you think this is like their version of sunscreen?" She shrugged her shoulders in response. We were both confused, so I picked up the bottle and turned it over to read the back. Searching the back of the bottle for the instructions, I figured out that it was skin bleach. Skin bleach? I had never heard of that before. I showed it to my friend, and she had never heard of such a thing either. I set it back down on the shelf and we continued searching for sunscreen, but something was nagging at me. I wanted to ask someone about the skin bleach.

We finished our shopping trip and made it back to the car of our coordinator, who is a black American living in Kenya. After I sat down in the backseat and buckled in, I leaned forward.

"Penny, I have a question."

The coordinator turned around in her seat, just enough to make eye contact with me.

"Yes?"

"Well, when we were looking for sunscreen, we found skin bleach. What is that?"

Unoffended, she turned around further in her seat and said, "Oh—first, you didn't buy it, did you? It is awful for your skin—especially for *your* skin."

I shook my head, so she continued.

"It is a problem in Kenya. Women, and sometimes men, want to have lighter skin. They want to look like the people they see on television and in the movies. The Western people. They see white as beautiful and black as ugly, so they buy that bleach and companies make tons of money."

"Oh," I said, as I sat back. "That is something new to me. Well, thank you for explaining." For the rest of the ride home, I was silent and thinking about what that meant. When we returned to where we were staying an hour later, I was still thinking about that conversation and experience, so I wrote a blog post.

Scene Jump Cut: September 8, 2006

While growing up in America, we are taught that black is bad. A guy dressed in black is bad. When it is dark outside, it is bad and scary. When something bad happens in a movie, the lights are usually off or it is nighttime outside. The idea of "black is bad" is instilled in us from a young age. We hear it on the news, we hear it in school, and we hear it everywhere around us. How does the American culture of "black is bad" infiltrate into the African culture? Westernization and globalization. Many commercials on Kenyan TV are American, and many times portray white people as good. However, not all of the "white is good" commercials are from America. Many of us saw commercials while we were on our homestays of a man and a woman at a party. The man does not want anything to do with the woman because she is too dark. Then, after using the lightening cream, he talked to her. This message shows that light skin is better (and will get you a man).

Kenyan children are even told that "black is bad." Our coordinator reflected on the fact that her daughter hears this. She said that, "this statement and mentality diminishes Kenyan children's self-esteem."

It is ironic in some way. Kenyans want to be lighter and people in the States want to be darker, with oils and lotions.

Scene Jump Cut: October 2006
Mombasa, Kenya

My third experience of "white is good" occurred on one sunny afternoon in Mombasa, while I was traveling back to the orphanage from the street boys' compound. The orphanage where I was staying was about two or three matatu rides from the street boys' compound, depending on the route of the day. The matatus ran on something similar to a bus system, but without as much guidance or documentation to help riders figure out where to go. Every matatu is almost always jam-packed with people inside, outside, and on top of the van. If you can fit or hold on, you can ride.

This specific afternoon, the streets were very crowded. Men were yelling out where the matatus were traveling to, and trying to attract riders. (I found out later that most of the men working the matatus pocketed the money they made, so it was essentially a commission business.) I was with one of the orphans, a young man who was about my age and who, now that he was finished with school, was working at the orphanage. We finally were able to push our way onto the matatu we needed and grabbed on. As soon as the driver, the money man, and the other passengers saw that I was riding in the matatu, everything slowed down. The van came to an abrupt stop, the money man of the matatu made the two men in the front get out and hold on, and I was instructed to sit in the front seat all by myself, with the driver.

Confused, I said, "No, no, it is okay. I will hold on." But they did not want to hear that. My companion, the young man who now worked for the orphanage, told me, "Just sit down. You are white—they are not going to let you do anything else. Just be quiet and sit there."

I was in shock. I was a minority in a country that still treated me like a person in the majority. I was put on a pedestal and I wanted off of it as soon as possible. But I complied and we made it back home safely.

The last experience happened a few weeks later, and was the combination of experiencing both a wedding and a funeral.

While I was getting ready to cook for the older girls in the orphanage compound, one of the residents came up to me and said, "I have something to ask you."

"Okay," I said, as I was kneading the *ugali* and starting the small fire stove for the *chipatis*.

"I have a friend who is getting married," she said. "Will you be in her wedding?"

I stopped what I was doing and turned to look at her. I must have looked shocked, because she quickly said, "Oh, it is okay. You will be in it.

I will be in it. We go tomorrow to get fitted. Come with me."

Knowing I could not offend her or her friend by declining, I agreed. I finished making dinner for the girls, and after dinner, I went into my room, pulled back the mosquito netting, and laid my head on the pillow. As I fell asleep, I thought, "Wow, a wedding! What an experience." This was not going to be my first Kenyan wedding—I had attended one earlier, with my Kenyan mother and father, while I was in Nairobi. But this would be the first Kenyan wedding I was in.

The next morning I woke up to banging on my bedroom door. Fatima, the girl who had told me about the wedding the night before, was loudly saying, "Come along, it is time! We have a long ways to go."

I quickly jumped out of bed, threw on some clothes and was out of my bedroom door, ready to catch the matatu with her.

Two hours and about five matatus later, we got off in front of a technical school. "We are here," she said.

By this point in my life in Kenya, I knew I just needed to go with the flow. I followed her through the front gate and walked past three or four buildings. We finally arrived at the last building on the compound, where her friend was standing at the door, waiting for us. We were ushered in and, through broken English and reading context clues, I figured out that this friend we met was in seamstress school and was the bride-to-be. She was measuring each of us and was planning to make all of the dresses as part of her schooling.

A few weeks later, the dress was ready and I was a bridesmaid in a Kenyan wedding. My duties included standing up in front of the church and collecting the offering. While I enjoyed myself in the whole experience, I do not know what went on for most of the day because of the language barrier. I tried to be a fly on the wall while also fulfilling all of my duties.

The same week of the wedding, I was taken to a funeral. One of the street boys, Chengo, had befriended me during my time in Mombasa. He would climb coconut trees and bring me a fresh coconut, walk me home from the market, and sit with me during dinner. This specific morning—the morning a few days after the wedding—he arrived at the orphanage gate and asked for me. The guard called for me, and I came to say good morning. Now, although Chengo and I were friends, understand that he spoke very broken English and I understood minimal amounts of Swahili, so our friendship consisted of multiple misunderstandings.

That morning at the gate, he invited me to his mother's village. She was very sick and he wanted me to meet her. (Yes, his biological mother was alive, but he was considered an orphan because he had been shunned from his house at a young age due to the cost of raising children.)

"Come meet Mama. Long trip. Matatu. You have shilling?" he said to me.

"Yes, okay," I said, nodding.

I followed him out of the gate and onto the street. We waited and waited for a matatu. Finally, one arrived that was headed in the direction we would be traveling, away from the city. I had never gone this way before, but I was ready for whatever adventure was in store.

Chengo and I made the trip out to his village via matatu. It was a long trip, but I was excited to meet his mother. I knew she would only be able to speak her tribal language, but smiling and nodding had gotten me this far while living in Kenya, and I was sure it would get me through today, also.

When we arrived, we got off the matatu and headed to the compound in the village that only his family lived in. We were stopped before we could make it all the way, though: A man stopped us, looked me over, and then began speaking to Chengo in another language. I felt pretty self-conscious at this point and didn't know what was going to happen next.

After the conversation between Chengo and the older man, I was led further into the village. Chengo sat me down on a bench next to one of the buildings.

"Wait," he said, motioning with his hands. So I waited.

Nearly 30 minutes later, Chengo came back. What I understood him as saying to me was, "Sick mother. Come see her." What was mistranslated was the fact that his mother was no longer sick, but had actually died that morning. Not knowing this yet, I followed Chengo into a small, one-room building. There were drapes pulled around a bed. Two women pulled them back and I saw Chengo's mother lying there, in a pose that looked like she was sleeping. One of the women said, "Dead."

I slowly turned toward the person who had said that word and realized what was happening. I was viewing a dead body in a one-room, dirt-floor building in a village in Kenya. I was unexpectedly at her funeral.

The next few hours are still a blur. I was in complete shock. She had died hours earlier; her older sons were out past the village, digging her grave, when Chengo and I arrived. They saw the matatu, and when they saw a white woman get off with Chengo, one of the brothers came to talk to him.

After seeing Chengo's dead mother, I remember a lot of singing, some crying, and Chengo helping to carry his mother's body to the gravesite. At that point in the afternoon—at the time of transporting the body—I was not allowed to participate. It appeared that only the men were participating in the carrying and burying. I sat on my wooden bench next to a shack in the shade and waited, much like I had that morning before meeting—or I guess, seeing—his mother. I waited for Chengo to come back to me after burying his mother. When he did, we were both solemn. We got on a matatu back to the city and did not speak during the entire ride.

Scene Jump Cut: September 2006
Boys' Home, Mombasa, Kenya

If you haven't already looked up the word *mzungu*, I am sure that, by this point in the chapter, you are wondering: What does that word mean? Here is my experience with the word *mzungu*.

Every day, whether I was walking down the street or working with the street boys, I heard, "*Mzungu!* Hey, *mzungu!*" or "*Mzungu*, how are you?" This roughly translates to, "White person! Hey, white person!" or "White person, how are you?"

At first, I thought nothing of the word. If you look up the term on the internet, it technically means "people of European descent," which I am. I was called *mzungu* on a daily basis by my host siblings, by the men on the matatus, and by the street boys. I figured they were just pointing out the fact that I was white. However, after about two months, I began to see and hear the word differently, depending on who was saying it.

My thoughts went to the idea that I would not say to a black person on the street, "Hey, black person!" Or, to a person of Asian descent: "Hey, Asian person!" As I began to question this, I also started having conversations with other white volunteers from all over the world and the Kenyan leadership at the drop-in center for street boys.

Then it happened. I walked into the drop-in center compound, pulling open the large, metal gates after traveling to the center on a matatu. As soon as I entered with the other two volunteers, we began to hear, "Hey, muzugu! Hey, muzugu!" The boys were yelling greetings to us. They were running up to us to tell us about their morning, their evening, their life. The joy on their faces brought joy to our hearts. We were where we were meant to be in that moment.

We followed the group of boys to the large room where they had all of their classes and Bible studies. Some of the boys had just finished breakfast, others were lying on mats to sleep, and some were messing around and roughhousing with each other.

Once we got the boys settled down, they began to talk about racism and what racism meant in other countries—specifically the countries where the three volunteers in front of them were from: the United States, Belgium, and Germany.

One tenacious boy in the group said, "I heard in the USA there is racism. That black people and white people can't even be in the same place or drink from the same drinking fountains." At first, we were all caught off guard. However, reflecting on the comment, we needed to realize that the books that were donated to Kenya, to the boys and to the orphanages, were the "throwaways" from the United States. So, yes, the information in most of the books was dated and did describe a country of segregation.

After recovering from the initial shock of the statement, an American volunteer who had entered the room during the conversation said, "Yes, you are right. There is racism in the United States. It is not that extreme anymore, but racism is still around."

The boy then turned to the German volunteer and said, "Germany is the most racist place of all of them." I don't know if he was trying to egg on the volunteer, but either way, the German volunteer abruptly turned to face the boy who made that statement. She wanted to set the record straight. "I don't know about that, but I'm not."

The conversation ended and the boys were shuffled off to their respective places around the compound; the white volunteers stayed put in the large room. We began to talk with one another about the conversation we had just engaged in with the boys. We also talked about the racism we were experiencing from the boys—specifically, being called *mzungus* after many months of working with them. It was our assumption that they knew our names by now.

After lunch, the boys gathered again in the big room and the German volunteer began to explain how the word "muzugu" made her feel. She felt as though the boys did not want her there because they were calling her a mean name—a name that was not hers. The Belgium volunteer then began to talk about respect, and what respect means when interacting with many people. One of the key points was that respect is calling someone by their name. The conversation continued for a little bit longer, with some Swahili translation thrown into the mix. After that conversation session, the term *mzungu* was not—in the case of the street boys, at least—used around us again.

Reflecting on this interaction, and specifically while writing this book, I am not sure how I feel. Who determines what respect is? The perceiver? Were those boys actually being disrespectful, or were they showing us that we were part of their community? I am still unsure.

My assignment in Kenya was meant to last for one year, but it was cut short when I contracted malaria. I had been a little bit depressed being away from my family, and therefore I stopped taking my malaria medicine. The mosquitos were rampant in Mombasa, though. My most vivid memory of malaria is when I was traveling in a truck to the airport. At one point I looked down at my arm and I could see, either in reality or in my delirium, the sweat streaming out of each of the pores on my arm.

When I finally arrived back to my parents, I was skinny, my hair was like straw from having been braided, and I was overwhelmed by the idea of returning to my life in the States—the choices, the fast-moving life, the getting well. But I was also given time to reflect on my time in a third-world country. From funerals to weddings, from hospital visits to making friends and feeding the hungry, I'd had a lifetime of experiences that would impact my life for years to come.

5

Contemporary Motherhood

"Just because my son is biracial and I love him beyond measure—I believe he is beauty on earth—does not mean that everyone sees him that way. Society fears him and I much accept that. I will never truly understand his experiences, but I can be his roots when his wings are clipped."

A white mother, 2018

"White people are hesitant to talk about race, at least at first. It is seen as rude because it's like, that is how you see me."

This American Life, podcast

Scene Jump Cut: 2009
Applebee's, Chicago suburbs

"So, if the baby is a girl, I will name it. If the baby is a boy, you will name it," I confidently stated.

I was sitting across the table from my boyfriend, Jay, at an Applebee's in a suburb of Chicago. We had only been together for a few months and had recently found out that I was pregnant. I was 22, and this would be my first child; he was 32, and this would be his second. We were eating burgers and drinking: I had a glass of water, and Jay had an alcoholic drink.

"Yes," he said. "Let's just do that now. If we have a boy, I want his name to be Ahmad." He picked up his burger and took a bite.

Setting down my glass of water, I said, "Okay"—though uneasily. I hadn't had time to process what was happening. I was unwed and pregnant by a man I barely knew. I was still in a bit of shock. However, I responded with a name for a girl. "If we have a girl, I want her name to be Ava." I said this confidently and unwaveringly. We had made a decision.

Jay agreed, and we continued eating our burgers and catching up on what was happening in our lives. We were beginning to plan our lives as parents, and during this conversation—as well as in the weeks leading up to this conversation—I knew in the back of my mind that I had to marry this man. I could not be a mother to a bastard child. My religious upbringing crept into my head, and although I obviously had had sex before I was married, I definitely couldn't bring a child into the world without being married. What would people think? A minister's daughter—no, the daughter of *two* ministers—having a biracial child, while unwed? I would later find out that my parents did not care about this—they just wanted me to be happy, with a healthy baby. Marriage did not need to happen in their minds.

Six months after this conversation at Applebee's, I was married to Jay and giving birth to our son, Ahmad. During the pregnancy I had planned and organized how I wanted to decorate Ahmad's room. I had decided on a Curious George theme, because we had many of those books and I loved the colors—bright red and bright yellow.

After months of planning, we had received and collected red and yellow blankets, toys and more books related to Curious George; to complement George, we had sock monkeys from toy stores. One day, one of my friends—a white friend—said to me, "Uh, Anni—you realize that this is kind of weird, right?"

We were sitting in my new condo, the one that Jay and I were renting together. We had just signed a one-year lease the week prior, and I was in the beginning stages of putting together the nursery. My friend had come over to help me, keep me company, and be there in case anything went wrong. I was far enough along in my pregnancy that people never wanted to leave me alone, just in case I went into labor.

"What do you mean, it's 'weird'? The red and yellow, or the fact that I want my child to love the idea of being curious in the world?" I said, albeit somewhat sarcastically, with a smile on my face. I looked up at her as I said that and she gave me a slight smile back. She was making the crib, putting sheets on and making sure it was nice and snug; I was sitting on the floor, unpacking boxes from both baby showers and our move.

My friend responded with a slight smile. "Anni. Do you know what people sometimes call black people, in a derogatory way?" Pausing for a brief moment, she said, "Monkeys."

Holy shit. The light bulb went off. In my head, I was saying every curse word I had in my vocabulary. What had I done? I was filling my son's room with stereotypes—a son who was not even born yet.

"Dammit," I said. "Why hasn't anyone said anything to me about this?" I was upset and mad. What was I doing?

My friend shrugged. "I don't know. I figured Jay would have said something."

"No, he didn't," I responded. "We have to take most of this down. I can keep the colors and the things that were made for him, but everything else has to go. I will change it to an animal theme so that there are monkeys with other animals. I cannot start out this way." As I was talking I was getting more and more frantic, and tears began to well up in my eyes.

My friend stared at me for a second and then began doing as I said. We worked the rest of the day, redoing my Curious George-themed creations to incorporate other animals with the red and yellow colors.

When Jay got home that night, I was waiting for him on the couch. He got home later than he had said he would, and as I was waiting, I was getting more and more agitated. When he finally walked in the door, I was at my tipping point. I loudly said, "Why didn't you tell me? Why didn't you say anything?"

Shocked, he stared at me, confused. "What?"

"Curious George, the monkey, as the theme of our son's room—a son who will be black because of you. Why did you not tell me?" I stood up from the couch and walked to the front door, where he was standing. I wanted him to tell me the truth, pay attention—and I wanted to see if he smelled like weed or booze, to know what type of night it was going to be.

"Oh, like it's racist? I didn't think about it, I guess. I thought you knew." His words were slurring and I could tell that he was about done for the night.

"No!" I said, louder this time. I pushed him in the chest to get his attention and to display my anger. "I did not know. Well, I mean, I do know the racism behind it. I didn't want that in our son's room. You should have keyed me in a little bit. That is your job in this relationship—point out this shit to me!"

Shrugging his shoulders, he slurred the word "sorry" and turned around, slowly shuffling back to the bedroom. He was going to pass out for the night and I was becoming more and more upset because of his indifference.

I yelled down the hall to him, as he closed the bedroom door: "Well, no thanks to you and your lame ass, I changed it all today so it would be animals, and not monkeys!" I am sure that everyone in our condo building could hear me yelling, but I didn't care. This was not our first fight, nor would it be our last.

Although I had misstepped when planning the nursery, the overall pregnancy itself was easy (though in truth, I didn't have anything to compare it to). I did have gestational diabetes, but I was able to manage it through diet. Outside factors in my life began to become more and more difficult for me to handle, though.

I had married and was going to have a baby with a man who was not only 10 years older than me, but who had grown up in a world completely different from my own. (Imagine the difference between the west side of Chicago and small-town Iowa.) Jay got a little violent when he was under the influence, which was most of the time. He self-medicated himself daily with alcohol and marijuana, and I later found out he had many other women on the side and was a prominent drug dealer in his neighborhood. Additionally, he was a musician and was often gone at night. I was young, naïve, and desired the life I had always imagined: the life I had grown up with; the family I'd had—the "dream" of being an adult. However, my life was not turning out that way.

Scene Jump Cut: Circa 1970s

Jay grew up on the west side of Chicago. He was his mother's first child and had been born when she was a teenager. His biological father was in and out of his life, juggling addictions and homelessness. His father was often seen on the side of the street begging for money and was part of one of the west side gangs, which therefore placed Jay in the gang through blood. Years later, when Jay was a young adult, his father died of gangrene.

During Jay's childhood, he and his mother stayed at various places. Sometimes his mother would leave him at family members' houses; other times he wouldn't know where he was going to stay for the night. At times Jay would not know where he was going after school or if he would have a bed to sleep in. When he was a teenager, his mother married a Chicago police officer.

Her new husband was a gruff man—a no-nonsense man. He would sometimes help Jay, such as when he needed a new winter coat. This man was not a true father figure, but helped when he could and/or wanted to. Jay's mother eventually went back to school and earned a degree; she became a CNA at a local hospital. Jay's childhood, with its lack of stability; absent father figure; and involvement in gang and drug activity all influenced his adult life. His childhood experiences impacted his role as a father figure, as well as his experience with people outside of his in-group—which included me. I was outside of his in-group.

When I first met Jay, I would describe him to family and friends as a "Bob Marley" look-alike. Jay had long dreadlocks and was a professional jazz musician. He had graduated from high school and, later, Shaw University. In his younger days he was a world traveler, and this had resulted in a Croatian daughter. In the time that I knew him, he hustled with side jobs. He often was broke, drinking Hennessey, and wandering the streets in the attempt to make money in the bars of Chicago. Much later, I realized that many of his stories and past experiences—both good and bad—were revisionist history, and a manipulation of what actually occurred in his life.

Scene Jump Cut: 2007

About a year prior to our wedding, Jay and I met at work. He was the band director for the after-school program and I was an early childhood teacher. We had somewhat pursued each other, and we had our first date within my first year of teaching at the school. After our first date, he began to hang out at my apartment more and more often. It was nice to have a companion, and it seemed like every experience with him was a brand-new adventure. Race became a part of my life—not for the first time, really, but in a big way—in a way I was not expecting. One of my biggest realizations was the fact that everyone truly does have racist tendencies, regardless of their race. I would hear black people yell at me on the street,

"Oh, honey, you have jungle fever, huh?" and I would see white people give me a curious look as I walked down the street holding Jay's hand.

A few weeks after we had started dating, I had gone out with some friends on a bar crawl. I was pretty drunk and rode the El home to meet him at my apartment. He was getting home from a gig he'd had earlier in the evening. We arrived at the red line stop at Belmont at the same time, and he helped walk me home. As we were walking past the Starbucks on the corner of Belmont and Halsted, on the north side of Chicago, a white woman came up to us, grabbed both of my shoulders, and looked me straight in the eyes. "Are you okay?" she asked. "Do you need help?" I remember looking at her, confused, and in my foggy mind, thinking, "What in the hell are you talking about, lady?"

I politely said that I was okay—that he was my boyfriend, and he was just helping me get home. She let me go, and Jay and I were on our way.

Scene Jump Cut: 2009

During my pregnancy, President Obama was elected as the first black president. I could not be more excited to be bringing my son into a country that was "past racism" (which we all know was a false assumption). On the night that President Obama was elected, he had planned to have his party in Grant Park—just a few miles from my apartment in Boystown. Jay had received tickets to attend the event in Grant Park and had invited me to join him. By this point I was five months pregnant and did not leave the house all that much, other than to go to work and go on walks at all hours of the night. I did not attend the event with Jay; I hated being around people at this point in my pregnancy, and I was afraid of the violence that might occur that night. While some people would be excited about a black president, others would be angry that a black man had just been elected.

That night, after Jay left for the event in Grant Park, I was sitting in my ground-level apartment on my black-and-white IKEA couch, just staring at the television. I was watching what was going on no more than two or three miles from where I was living. Sitting on the couch that night, I was ecstatic. I watched Barack, Michelle, and their two little girls walk out on stage. Michelle, in her beautiful black-and-red dress; Barack, in a suit; and their girls, in beautiful dresses. I sat there and stared at the screen, rubbing my belly—my belly that had a biracial son inside. My son would be born when our country had a black president, a president who looked like him.

Although I was happy, sitting alone in my apartment that night, I cried. I cried because I believed that I understood the magnitude of what was happening. I also apprehended, maybe for the first time, that my son would not be seen as "my" son—the son of a white woman—when he walked the streets. He would be seen as a black man, just like people saw Barack Obama as a black man. My son would have women move to the other side of the street when they saw him walking toward them. My son would have people call him derogatory names. My son would be a socially perceived black man in America, with all of the positives and negatives that come along with that identity. I was scared, as his mother—his white mother. How would I make sure that I could protect him, prepare him for a racist world, and help him become a strong man who did not fall into a negative stereotype?

A few months after President Obama's election, Jay and I awoke early for my scheduled cesarean section. My son was in the breech position and there was not enough room to try to turn him, so about a month before his due date, the doctors scheduled a C-section for exactly one week before my due date. Additionally, I was on minimal health insurance—this was before Obamacare—and since I'd had the minimum amount of doctor's appointments and ultrasounds necessary, the doctors saw me as a "poor white woman" and treated me as such.

The morning of the delivery, I picked up the bag that I had packed the night before and walked behind Jay to our gray Jeep Cherokee, parked in front of our condo. Jay was in the driver's seat and drove us the 50 blocks to the place where I would give birth, the Norwegian American Hospital.

We arrived at the hospital around 6:30 a.m. on March 9, and Jay parked in the parking lot before walking me inside. We went to where we were instructed to go, checked in, and were guided to another part of the hospital.

Once I checked in at the labor and delivery desk, the nurses handed me a hospital gown to change into and hooked me up to machines. They checked my insulin levels, my heart rate and the baby's heart rate, and asked many questions: Had I had anything to eat after midnight? Did I need to use the bathroom? Finally, the nurses hooked up a machine that had a belt that would wrap around my belly.

"Do you know that you are in labor?" the nurse asked me, as the machine began beeping.

"No. I mean, I am just uncomfortable."

"Sweetheart, you are having contractions," she said in a matter-of-fact tone.

Shrugging my shoulders, I said, "Oh, well, I guess it is good we have a C-section soon." I smiled slightly, not knowing exactly what that meant at the time. Thankfully, the rest of the procedure went smoothly.

When it was time to have my son, the hospital staff rolled me into the operating room. Jay stood at the head of the bed/operating table. They dropped a sheet down to cover my stomach from view and I grabbed Jay's hand, gripping his fingers harder than I had ever gripped anything. I was nervous and scared. He would complain that I messed up his thumb that day until the last time that I saw him, in 2011.

Once the sheet was down, the doctor asked, "Can you feel this?"

I looked at her, confused, and said, "Can I feel what?"

She laughed and said, "Okay, it's time to have a baby."

After that moment, I do not remember a whole lot. I remember that when they pulled my son out, I kept saying, "Why do I not hear him? Why do I not hear him?" But then his cry rang out.

Before wheeling me to recovery and Ahmad to the nursery, they held him up for me to see. He had a full head of hair. He was beautiful.

Once I was in the recovery room, I did not get to see my son. I was confused. No one told me what was going to happen. They saw me as an unmarried, poor mother. (I had not changed my name or marital status at the doctor's office because the paperwork was overwhelming.) Television shows mothers getting to bond with their babies right away—why couldn't I? I was getting more and more anxious when I realized that I was hooked up to a blood pressure machine. I figured out a way to get so agitated that the machine spiked and made a noise, which got the attention of the nurses. The nurse came running over to check on me. I do not know what I said, but the next thing I knew, my mom was standing next to my recovery bed.

Months later, I found out that Jay had my glasses and was nowhere to be found, and that when the nurse went out to the waiting room asking for "Mr. Krummel," my dad had stood up. My mom, realizing what was happening, told him to sit down and went with the nurse. She stood by my side during my recovery, comforting me while she was internally steaming and livid at Jay for disappearing.

Hours after the C-section and recovery, I was rolled into my own suite. Trying to make up for the fact that he had disappeared, Jay flirted with the nurses in the attempt to get me my own room and to bring my son to me. It had been at least two hours since I gave birth and I still had not seen Ahmad, other than the initial "Oh, here is your baby" moment in the operating room. At that moment, Jay's actions made up for his disappearance, in my book. He got me my own room because he knew I "wouldn't do well in a shared room," and he got my son to me.

That afternoon, my sister, parents, and friends came by to meet my new son. I was still somewhat numb from the hips down and needed assistance to go to the bathroom. After meeting Ahmad and talking to me for a little while, everyone began to leave. First my friends left, then my parents and sister left (they rode together), and then Jay left.

"What? You are just going to leave me here, Jay? I still can't get up by myself." I was upset, but didn't have the fight in me that day.

"They will take care of you. I will go talk to the nurses," he said. And that was the last I saw of him that night.

I was left in the room with my newborn son, who was only hours old, unable to really go to the bathroom by myself, at 23 years old. What the hell was happening to me? I was alone. I got through that night with the help of nurses, and a lot—I mean *a lot*—of self-talk.

The nurses, feeling pity, took my new baby for the evening and watched him in the nursery so that I could get some sleep. I vividly remember talking to myself as I shuffled slowly to the bathroom that night, because I hated to ask for help.

The next day, Jay came back and my son was back in the room with us. Where had Jay gone that night? Where had Jay gone during the recovery period? I have never asked, and to be honest, I do not want to ask, because I know his answer will be a lie. I imagine that he was at his girlfriend's house—a girlfriend I found out about months later—or out hustling a gig.

How long did I stay in the hospital? I do not actually remember. I think I stayed two nights—both spent alone. In the days and months since March 9, 2009, I have become confident in my personal strength and know that it goes far beyond the limitations of my mind.

Until the birth of my son, I never truly understood the saying "It takes a village." But, wow—does it ever. I do not know what I would have done without Ms. Reese. She was my rock through hard times, my son's pseudo-grandma when I needed a night off, and a loving person who dedicated her life to children. She taught me about Ahmad's hair when he had cradle cap; she fed him rice cereal when he wouldn't stay full. She was there when I needed someone to talk to, to understand me, and to just listen. She was also there for my son—something I can never repay her for.

Ms. Reese was a widow and a matriarch in West Chatham, a neighborhood in Chicago around 76th and Vincennes, when I met her in 2009. At the time I knew her, she was in her 70s and raising her developmentally disabled adult son, who lived in the basement, and an adopted teenage daughter. I met Ms. Reese through Jay, who grew up around the street from her when he lived with his grandma. Ms. Reese had raised half the neighborhood, including my son's cousin, who was a few years older than he.

Ms. Reese was a strong, black woman who kept an iron bar behind the door for safety reasons. She viewed her ability to help raise the children of the neighborhood as a calling—something she could do for "her children," to make money, and to help out the single moms who needed the assistance, guidance, and moral support. Her prices were cheap, her care was loving, and her dedication to the growth of all of her children was beyond measure.

Below is an open letter to Ms. Reese—my "village." It is a personal reflection and blogpost, from 2017:

Dear Ms. Reese,

Thank you. Thank you for your wisdom, your songs, your stories, your ability to raise my son, and your willingness to be a mentor and a person I could rely on in a time when there were few other people within a 30-mile radius to help me raise my son.

You are a rock. You are a matriarch. You are a woman who has protected, raised, and watched over "your kids" for generations. I still think back on the stories you used to tell me about coaching all the neighborhood kids in baseball, running the streets and making them all play, and ensuring that "your kids" stayed out of trouble. I admired your frankness in keeping an iron crowbar behind your door for the "crazy people in the street." I can still see my young infant/toddler son light up when he saw you, ate your Ritz crackers, and chewed on a chicken leg while you sang, cooked, and made him feel as if he was one of yours. I also can still remember the devastated look on my son's face when his father did not show up in the morning to watch him. However, I knew you were my constant. I knew that no matter what, you would take my son that day, love him, and help him forget about his deadbeat father.

We educated each other. You taught me when to add rice cereal (probably a little too early) to my son's bottle and I taught you the NEED to put sunscreen on a biracial baby's skin.

Since the day I met you, I knew I wanted to be a woman like you in my older age. At 72 years old I still want to be able to get on the floor to show the young ones how to dance and stretch, but also be as wise as you: A woman who helped single moms, moms in distress, moms who didn't understand what the hell the men in their lives were doing. You let me leave my son at your house overnight when I just needed "me time." You only made me pay $20 a day (a steal, for how long he was with you). You helped the poor, single, stressed out, young moms that needed someone to be there for their kids and for them—and you were. I don't think I can ever repay you enough.

I still tell people that my son is so smart because, for the first 18 months of his life, he was constantly talked to, loved, held, sang to, and pushed to be the best. And he is the best.

Over the years we have lost touch, but I think about you often. You left a mark on my life, and I want to say "thank you."

Scene Jump Cut: February 2010

Before Ahmad's first birthday, I had had enough. Jay had emptied my bank account, I had heard from several people—including his so-called girlfriend—that he was not being loyal, and he was more and more into drugs and alcohol than I would have liked. There had already been several nights when I had threatened to call the police, and one night, I even had to. There had already been multiple times when I would run, with Ahmad in my arms, to our bedroom, slamming the door shut and lying over him in the fetal position in order to protect him from his own father. Overall, Jay was not always the nicest person and I was unhappy. At the age of 23, I knew I could be happy; I knew I deserved to be happy, so I filed for divorce.

The divorce process took more than a year and included emergency hearings, times when Ahmad and I would run away to a hotel with my mother, to stay safe, and many yelling matches. However, it was eventually finalized in the week my maternal grandmother passed away. The divorce ended when Jay had all of his fight taken away. The divorce was inevitable, and he knew it. It only took him one more year to become the absent father, which confirmed biases for many people in my life.

In more recent years— and while writing this book, specifically—I began reflecting on Jay's abandonment of Ahmad. Now, to some readers, this insight may "go too far"— which it might—but it gave me something to chew on. Today, I continue to grapple with the fact that Jay signed over his paternal rights to my current husband, Doug.

For generations—hundreds of years—black men were taken from their families, sold, and sometimes never heard from again. They were stripped from the fabric of family life, leaving strong women behind to raise their children. While this history is not an excuse, it does begin to help comprehend the psychology—as least for me—behind why black fathers so often leave their children behind. It helps me understand Jay from a different mindset, and while it may not be accurate, it provides me with a possible explanation for the abandonment.

While listening the podcast, *This American Life*, I heard my own voice in the voice of a black mother raising her black son: "I am afraid to raise a black son. There is only a little bit of time when people see black boys as cute. There is an even larger amount of time (most of their lives) that people see black men as threatening." I am afraid. I am afraid of how society will see my son. I am afraid of how society will treat him. I am afraid that I am not preparing him to live in a racist world.

Motherhood is hard, and the path to motherhood can be different for many people. As Ahmad continues to grow and make friends, I am always curious, always questioning situations. Earlier, I described my eagle-like eyes that are always focused on how people interact with Ahmad in new or old situations, and how I have yet to find a group with which to discuss the motherhood challenges specifically related to raising a black son. However, other situations also come into play. I listen to the conversations Ahmad has with his friends during car rides or video game marathons. I watch how his cousins interact with him, and my red flags rise often. When should I speak up? Does Ahmad realize what is happening? As he gets older, I think he does understand—and my job of engaging in conversations, with him as a black boy with predominately white friends and cousins who have grown up in a racist society, is the next step in my learning and growing process.

6

Race and Police

Scene Jump Cut: 2009
Southshore neighborhood, Chicago

Hiding in the corner with my son wrapped tightly in my arms, I dialed my cell phone as I heard a *pop, pop, pop* outside. This noise was not fireworks; it was the sound of gunshots, right outside our windows.

The phone was ringing. "Pick up—*please*, pick up." I couldn't tell if I was saying it out loud or in my head, but I wanted Jay to pick up the damn phone. Finally, after the fourth or fifth ring, I heard, "Hello?" Music was blaring in the background, as if he was at a bar or pub.

"They are doing it again. You have to come home now!" I said frantically. My heart was racing, my mind was running wild, and my body was in overload. I was out of my element; I had to be in a dream.

"Are you safe? Where are you? I am way up on the north side, but I will call the police," he said calmly. I don't know if he was used to this happening, or if he was too stoned/drunk to care about his family, but this was the second or third time this week I had called him late at night while gang members rang shots around our condo. They were in the middle of a turf war, and our condo was smack-dab in the middle. When we signed the lease we had not realized that it was in the middle of two gangs' territories, but we had figured it out all too soon.

"Get the f*** home *now*!" I said, on the verge of tears and with my teeth gritted. "You need to be home right now." I was irate. I was scared. I was sitting in the dark with my infant son in my arms, trying to protect both of us from the gunshots that were firing outside.

Jay showed up at the condo about three hours later. By that point, Ahmad and I had survived the shooting and had fallen asleep in the hallway on some blankets and pillows. (Why the hallway? Because it was away from all of the windows in the condo.) When Jay got home, he did not wake Ahmad or me. He just passed out on the couch after eating Little Debbie snacks, which I only assumed later from the packages that were lying around him on the floor. It had been a normal night for him.

Later the next morning, Jay woke up and I was still mad. "What the hell? What took you so long to come home?"

"I was home, Anni. I was outside, talking to Dude about all the shooting. His car got hit with a bullet last night." (Dude was our neighbor across the street.) Jay was still lying on the couch, shirtless and reeking of alcohol.

"Well, you should have been home!" And with that I stomped back to the bedroom to get Ahmad ready for the day.

After a few months of living on the South Side, I realized that it was not only the gangs we had to fear, but sometimes the police, too. I began to understand the type of fear Jay tried to instill in me, living on the South Side of Chicago with a socially perceived black son. Most of the time, I had no idea what he was talking about when he would say things like, "They are out to get us" or "Watch your back, you don't know who is out there." I thought he was joking or paranoid most of the time. In relation to police, I was under the impression (from my own childhood and lived experiences) that police were there to help and protect the people of a community. Police were supposed to be nice men and women, who have

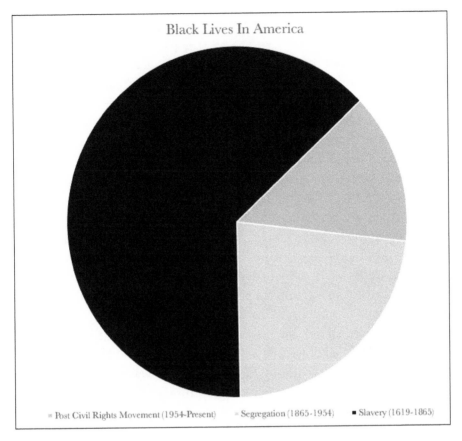

the goal of protecting and enforcing laws for the common good. That, I realized, is not the case when you live in a predominately black area— especially in Chicago, which is arguably one of the most segregated areas of the United States.

Growing up as a white female, I had always appreciated and trusted the police force. However, after reading books, listening to people and podcasts, and doing a little bit of my own research, I realized that trust in the police is not a feeling that everyone in America shares. Through research, I learned that the original purpose of the police was to protect white people from black people. Police were designed to ensure that black people did not run away from their owners—or, in later years, drink from the water fountains of white people. In today's world, with the murder of multiple people of color at the hands of police officers, the lack of trust in communities of color is still there, regardless of the police officer's skin color.

I have learned that many people of color, as well as social justice activists, believe that through the implicit biases of being raised in America and/ or through some of the police training, police officers are taught to still protect and serve *only the whites*. Historically, police officers have been seen by white people as an institution in the community that they can trust; in communities of color, police officers are seen as oppressors. This concept relates back to the first chapter—of police putting their hands on people of color more often in traffic stops, of killing more black people during minor offenses, and so forth. Considering the institution of policing and understanding the history of policing, it is important to comprehend the deep-seated, differing views of police officers when controversies such as Black Lives Matter vs. Blue Lives Matter become prominent in the United States. A little (or a lot) of truthful history can provide a better foundation for discussions.

One afternoon, on our way home from a family event at Jay's cousin's house, we were driving down one of the streets on the South Side—maybe at 74th or at 95th. It was around dusk and the sun was setting behind the clouds. There was a police car following us, though I didn't notice it until Jay pointed it out to me.

He said something to me along the lines of, "Be cool, Anni. We got the cops behind us. You never know what they are going to do to us down here."

Confused, I furrowed my eyebrows and turned to face him from the passenger seat of our Jeep. "To us? What are you talking about? You are crazy." At this point, I whipped my head around to look at the police car following us. I did not think twice about it.

Immediately, Jay—in a low but stern voice—said, "Anni, dammit, you don't understand. They are going to think we are doing something wrong and pull us over. Sit still, don't move, and just don't bring attention to us."

With that reaction from Jay, a lightbulb clicked on in my head. I finally realized the intense fear he had internalized all of his life, which I had not learned, felt, or even realized, as a white woman in America.

A few weeks later, it was Jay's first Father's Day with Ahmad and we had decided to visit one of his friends at his apartment. We were going to grill and spend the afternoon together. We arrived and were welcomed with a smiling face and the smell of meat already cooking.

Jay and his friend went outside to put the last pieces of meat on the grill while Ahmad and I sat on the couch in the living room. Jay and his friend came back in and made side dishes in the kitchen, while Ahmad and I looked on. All of the sudden, we heard yelling and (what I thought were) fireworks, right outside the door. It was a holiday, so I figured, "Oh, fireworks for all holidays, down here on the South Side." However, it was not fireworks—it was gunshots. Once I realized what was happening, Jay and his friend were already hiding in the kitchen, leaving Ahmad and I on the couch, right by the front door. I did not have time to get up. I just froze.

After the shots faded away, we all went outside to see what had happened. Someone had obviously called 911, because we could hear sirens coming. We all turned to the right and saw the person who had been gunned down. No one moved. Jay said, "Do not touch him. They will be here soon. If you touch him, whoever shot him will be after you next."

Minutes later, I sat on the front stoop with my black son on my lap, watching a Chicago police officer stand over a young black boy who was bleeding to death in front of him. Jay was yelling at the officer, "Sir—*sir*! You are supposed to do something! You know CPR. Why are you not helping him?" The police officer heard him, looked away and kept on with whatever he was doing, which was not helping the dying boy lying in front of him.

The police officer—a man who was supposed to protect and serve—blatantly let a black boy die from gunshot wounds right in front of us, and on someone else's lawn—someone who did not know him. Then, it was like a spotlight was placed on me. In slow motion, every police officer on the block turned and saw me, the only white person within hollering distance. A white, female police officer—probably a detective—walked purposefully toward me, though not too quickly. She could see that we had been grilling, but was not aware that at the exact moment the shots were fired, we had been inside the apartment. How could she know? She saw us, with a grill, and she figured we knew something. But, honestly, we didn't.

When my husband and his friend saw the white female police officer walking toward us, they began saying, "Gurl, she's coming for you. White girl gonna try to talk to your ass. You betta …" I was so confused. Two minutes ago I was sitting on the couch in the living room, with my son on my lap. I heard gunshots, froze, and then went outside to see what the shouting was about. My husband, his friend, and I saw a boy die in front of us— and no one had helped, not even the police officer. And now, she was going to get me? Get me for what?

When the police officer got close enough to touch me, she looked me straight in the eyes, lowered her voice, and leaned in. Her words came out slowly, and I was unsure of what was happening. She said, "Come on, you know you saw it. What happened?" In my mind, she ended that comment with a wink, but I don't know if that actually happened or not. It was like she had cued in on me because I was "like her," and *of course* I would tell her everything, because we were in the same "group."

In my head, I was thinking, be quiet. You saw nothing. I was also thinking, What in the world is this lady doing? We are all standing out here. I just watched her fellow officer let a young boy die, and now she wants to pressure me to tell her something that I don't know? Finally, words came out of my mouth and I said, "We did not see anything. We were inside." She continued to question me a bit but realized that I either wasn't going to talk or really did not know anything, and so she walked away.

Scene Jump Cut: 2016-2018

Close to 10 years after those incidents with Jay on the South Side of Chicago, we are in a national moment called Black Lives Matter. White people are finally realizing that black people are being murdered by police, and the conversation is changing. At the end of a blog post in July of 2016—after the murder of Alton Sterling, Philando Castile, and so many others—I wrote this as my reflection of the current times:

> *After this last police murder of Alton Sterling (and now Philando Castile), I lay in bed, thinking, What would I say at a news conference, if that were my son? What would I say in a news conference to help people understand that not all perceived black people fit whatever stereotype you have formed in your head? How would most of America react if a white woman stood up and cried for her black son? This may be my white privilege coming out, or it might be the fact that I*

should not sit up (or wake up) crying because people who are supposed to protect him killed another person who looks like him. I taught my son, at a young age, that police are there to help. Whenever he saw a police officer as a toddler, he would look up at me and say, "Mommy, I wonder who they are going to go help now?" But, are they? Was that the right thing to teach him? I hope so.

So what now? As a mother of a black son, who has no life experience to base my conversations with him on—only word of mouth and books—I need to become educated and stand up. However, how much does my voice matter? How many people will listen? To the world, I am just another white woman who is trying to stand up for black people. But to me, I am a white woman who is fighting for her son, a black boy.

I tell myself often that race is not real. It is a visible social construct, developed over the centuries as a means to identify individuals based on skin color. However, race is prominent. One's race cannot be invisible, and to society, it is real; it is how people are described by others and how people describe themselves. It is how police officers depict suspects and (statistically) determines how a traffic stop is going to progress.

Recently, a participant in a study I was conducting described how she looked in a video. She wanted to view her videos as part of a reflection piece, and therefore, I needed to find her video in the file filled with 100 other videos. At first, I just could not remember which participant she was. In an email, she stated, "I have caramel skin, my hair is pulled back, and I have glasses." The fact that she stated her skin color first was eye-opening for me. We teach our children that skin color is just one more thing about a person, but we do not use it to label a person. However, sometimes people self-describe, and those explanations begin with skin color. Even while interviewing my father for this book, we were talking about skin color and he stated, "I try to consciously not describe someone by their skin color."

Race is not based in any science. Race has changed over the generations. At one time in our history, Irish people were seen as another "race," before other people began coming to America and Irish people were accepted as part of the "main (white) race." People with more melanin were dehumanized. While race is not based in science, it is anything but dead in the lives of the American people. It is, in fact, very much alive. We are all products of a racialized society. Regardless of what race we are perceived as, it is arguably the biggest indicator of our success in life. If a black person can "pass" as white, their success in life is measurably different—usually for the better—than their family counterparts who may have a darker skin tone. Skin color is a determining fact in everyone's life, whether you want to realize it or not. It ranges from white privilege to the dehumanizing actions and words received by people of color.

Race is also based in language. Words—specifically, words used toward people of color—began in oppressive roots. The pain that accompanies the words that have, for generations, diminished the lives of people of color, can be felt deeply and should be recognized as such.

"Sticks and stones may break my bones, but words will never hurt me." While that old saying may be true for some, for others, words can dig deep into the soul. Language will not only lift up or push down people; it will also provide power and control. The learning of language and the ability to read changes the trajectory of people. Language holds power, and language can construct or destruct a power structure.

Language is so powerful—and the way people "sound" is so powerful—that people make judgments based on the tone, volume, and location of sounds in one's mouth. While listening to a podcast, *Code Switch*, I learned about an African-American, male news anchor who goes to speech therapy because he places words with "th" sounds in the back of his mouth, does not open his mouth fully when speaking, and consequently sounds "less intelligent" or "black" to the management at television stations. He, along with many news anchors, goes to school and speech therapy in order to sound more "white"; to sound more "Midwestern." As one of the hosts said, "people sound all kinds of colors"—but you need to sound the "right" color in a racialized and classist America.

Words.

Words, whether they are spoken, nonverbal, or perceived, interact in a way in our lives that is constant, daily, and impossible to ignore. Words have meaning, regardless if you understand or agree with the meaning or not. Additionally, not all words are defined by their dictionary definitions. With the invention of Urban Dictionary, I believe that this generation understands that concept completely. Words can be positive or negative.

Words can be uplifting or oppressive. Words, when it comes to racism, usually boil down to name-calling: the name-calling of white people with words like "cracker" and of black people with the N-word—a word that is described in Urban Dictionary as:

1. A racist term used to describe any dark-skinned people, but generally reserved for those of African descent.
2. A term used by incredibly ignorant black people to describe themselves, but considered racist when used by non-blacks.
3. *Carte blanc* (temporary relationship separation) to black people to beat non-blacks into a coma when used publicly.
4. A secret code word to be used by whites who desire quick, free, total dental extractions at the hands of unlicensed, amateur, black dentists.

Webster's Dictionary (online version, 2018) also defines the usage of the N-word:

> *Nigger is an infamous word in current English, so much so that when people are called upon to discuss it, they more often than not refer to it euphemistically as "the N-word." Its offensiveness is not new— dictionaries have been noting it for more than 150 years—but it has grown more pronounced with the passage of time. The word now ranks as almost certainly the most offensive and inflammatory racial slur in English, a term expressive of hatred and bigotry. Its self-referential uses by and among black people are not always intended or taken as offensive (although many object to those uses as well), but its use by a person who is not black to refer to a black person can only be regarded as a deliberate expression of contemptuous racism.*

When reading or hearing the words "cracker" or "n*****," which one is worse? Are they both bad? Which word was designed to oppress? Is it evident in how I wrote the words, and how news organizations write the two words when having conversations during talk segments? One is derogatory and one is not. One is used by people in power, and one is often seen as a joke.

But then, the question becomes: Well, if black people can say n*****, then why can't I (a white person)? Because you do not get to have access to everything. White people are so used to the world being theirs, and—well, this word is not ours. I do not say this word aloud, and as is evident in this book, I do not write it. I do not have power in this word. The N-word has power—more power than what is depicted in the dictionary definition: "a contemptuous term for a black or dark-skinned person." The word n***** was invented to oppress, to put slaves "in their place." There is pain associated with the term. There is deep-seated hurt, abuse, embarrassment, and worthlessness. The word n*****, along with other derogatory terms invented by and used by white people as a way to show power over people of color, victimized a set of people—a set of people that were enslaved for over 200 years.

Two hundred years of grandparents never setting foot on free soil—instead, being beaten and called a n*****. So, white people, no—we do not have access to that word. We do not have access to that word either alone or with other words, even if it is a common saying. If you research, the pain—the derogatory sayings, songs, and marketing materials associated with the word—your mouth might open in shock, as mine did during this portion of my own growth. The point of growth that stuck out to me the most was a children's story called "The Ten Little N****s," which was later changed to *Ten Little Indians* (which is also quite problematic).

> *Ten Little N***** Boys went out to dine;*
>
> *One choked his little self, and then there were nine.*
>
> *Nine Little N***** Boys sat up very late;*
>
> *one overslept, and then there were eight.*
>
> *Eight Little N***** Boys traveling in Devon;*
>
> *one said he'd stay there, and then there were seven.*
>
> *Seven Little N***** Boys chopping up sticks;*
>
> *one chopped himself in halves, and then there were six.*
>
> *Six Little N***** Boys playing with a hive;*
>
> *a bumblebee stung one, and then there were five.*
>
> *Five Little N***** Boys going in for Law;*
>
> *one got in Chancery, and then there were four.*

Four Little N***** Boys going out to sea;

a Red Herring swallowed one, and then there were three.

Three Little N***** Boys walking in the zoo;

the big bear hugged one, and then there were two.

Two Little N***** Boys sitting in the sun;

one got frizzled up, and then there was one.

One Little N***** Boy living all alone;

he got married, and then there were none.

So, the word n***** is not in white vocabulary because of the history and pain associated with it. No, we cannot have access to it. No, it is not unfair.

Yes, race influences our lives. Yes, discussing race is an uncomfortable and sometimes heated topic. Yes, black people and people of color are treated different when police see them in public, pull them over, or pass them on the streets. But my question—my reflection on race and police—is this: Where does my voice fit? I am a white mother of a socially perceived black son. Many white people do not talk about race because that is part of the privilege in America; not talking about race is fine because "it doesn't influence our lives." But it does.

I am not asking to be the center of a conversation, but just an additional member, a fly on the wall—someone who is able to hear what black families are talking about to their black sons. I want to be able to ask questions, so I can educate my son in this world of fear and joy. I long to be part of a larger conversation that people may not initially perceive me to be part of—but I am. I am raising a black boy in a world of racism. Where do I fit into the community of mothers and fathers raising sons of color without feeling shunned or judged? In a community of white parents raising children of color? In a community of parents of color, raising children of color? Or is it a combination of these communities? Maybe I don't need a voice, but I do need to listen to and feel part of a community so that I, as well as other parents who are raising children of color, feel support. My life experiences do not and will not reflect my son's, but how do I escort him through life, as an advocate and guide?

7

Identity

*"The name Ahmad is an Arabic baby name. In Arabic, the meaning of the name Ahmad is **much praised**. One of many names of the Prophet Muhammad."*

SheKnows.com, baby names website

"They considered themselves white, but DNA tests told a more complex story."

The Washington Post, Feb. 6, 2018

Scene Jump Cut: 2009

By 2009, I was pregnant and in the planning stages of having a son. I often engaged in conversations with my parents about my upcoming delivery, life, and child. On this specific day, my mom and I were talking on the phone as I sat in my dirty basement apartment, smelling the scent of incense that was streaming through the windows.

Holding the phone to my ear, I heard my mom say, "Anni, are you *sure* you want to use that name? Don't you think there would be a better name to choose? Don't you think you might want to pick a more *Christian* name?"

We were talking about my upcoming wedding to Jay and I was also relaying to her that I was having a boy. Jay and I had decided on names early on in the pregnancy, and "Ahmad" was the name we would be giving a boy.

Quite annoyed, I was blunt in my response. "Yes, Mom. 'Ahmad' is the name we picked. His middle name is going to be 'LeDrew,' like dad." I took a deep breath and sat down on my large black-and-white couch.

"Okay, Anni. I just want to make sure you take time to think about it." The tone of her voice told me that she was backing down. She knew that she was not going to change my mind in this conversation.

I needed to pace now. I stood up and began pacing around my (very) small kitchen, smelling the incense that was burning by the window.

"Okay, I understand, Mom," I said shortly.

As the conversation continued I could sense the discomfort, disapproval, and maybe even slight sadness in her voice. I am sure that my life was not taking the path she had hoped for me. I am sure that her sadness, disapproval, and shock were supported by worries that kept her awake at night. I just could not understand her worry in my early 20s. As a fifth-generation Presbyterian, I had learned and embodied the idea that Christianity is a practice of love and acceptance—not judgment and discrimination. Eventually, my mother said, "You know he is going to have a hard time as he gets older with that kind of name." I still didn't fully understand it.

Nearly 10 years after that phone call—when I first relayed the name of my new baby to my mother— I have begun to understand her worry. People judge a book by its cover—and by its name. I have become acutely aware of the prejudices that exist based on both visible and invisible factors. There have been events, mindsets, and statements made about people with names that sound like (or are) Ahmad's in our country since his birth.

This concept hit home when, one day, I saw a news story about a 14-year-old boy named Ahmed Mohamed. Ahmed was arrested for creating a clock and showing it to his teacher, who mistook it for a bomb. It can be assumed that the teacher's implicit bias came into play and, therefore, the police were called. Ahmed was handcuffed. News articles showed a picture of Ahmed, handcuffed and with his hands behind his back, a confused and worried look on his face.

So, what is in a name? Prejudices. Preconceived notions. Biases.

After President Trump was elected, I became even more scared about my son's identity and how his identity would be viewed in the wider world.

During his first few months in office, President Trump signed an executive order (which was later denied) designed to prevent anyone from specified Muslim countries from entering the United States.

I, along with a majority of American citizens, began watching what was happening in airports around the country. Lawyers were sitting on airport floors, trying to help people who were in the air when the order was signed. Airport officials were not just holding people from Muslim countries against their will, but also people who looked Muslim or had names that were of Muslim origin. While all of this was happening, I did not share any of my fears with my family—yet I wonder if they had the same silent thoughts. What would this mean for Ahmad? The next time we intended to fly, was something going to happen to him? Would his name make him stand out?

In the coming months, we had several flights already booked, including one to Florida for a Disney Cruise to the Bahamas. Whether my fears were rational or irrational, I had plans A, B, and C all in place for when we traveled.

So, what's in a name? Identity.

I admit that I have occasionally contemplated changing Ahmad's name to Drew (a variation of his middle name), just to make things easier for him. But then I question this thought: Why change who he is just to make everyone else feel comfortable? If he chooses to change his name or go by a different name one day in his life, I will support that, but I am not going to make the decision for him. A name gives you an identity.

Identity and a connection to family is often what a name provides. I am named after my two grandmothers. My dad is a junior, and named directly after his father. My mother is named after her grandmother. As is evident, names within my family bear an identity and a connection to who you are, as is the case in many families. Therefore, my son was named by his father in a loose connection to his favorite pianist, Ahmad Jamal. Ahmad was also given the middle name of my father, thereby carrying on the Krummel male middle name. This connection to generations past provides both a history and an identity.

Ahmad's middle name is that of his paternal great-grandfather and grandfather. The story in our family about the name "LeDrew" began when my grandfather was born, in the 1930s. As the story goes, his mother—while reading the newspaper—came across the name "LeDrew" in the convictions and arrests section. My great-grandmother loved that name and decided to give it to my grandfather as a middle name. The name was then passed on to my father, and from there was passed on to my son. A name incorporates history, interesting stories, and a connection.

Unfortunately, names also provide a reason for people to make judgments. Just like airline officials were pulling people out of line who had "Muslim-sounding" names, human resource departments also display prejudices based on names. "Every day, a black-name resume is 50 percent less likely to get responded to than a white-name resume. That's everyday racism." (Jalen Ross, CNN, 2015) Additionally, if a person of color is offered a job position and accepts—and the job setting is predominately white—a common practice is "tone policing." Tone policing, in reference to this example, is when a predominately white staff instruct black coworkers to "not get so defensive," or "quiet down." While discrimination based on name and tone policing does not happen in every context, it will occur, statistically, more often than not. As a white person in a work environment, it is always good to question personal internalized stereotypes, to reflect, and to ask yourself if the judgment you made is a fair judgment to make. I can tell you from experience that, usually, it is not.

Interestingly, many years after naming my son with the last name "Mayfield" and getting divorced, I realized that my son still bore his biological father's maternal last name, and not his paternal last name. While dating and going through the marriage process, I never questioned or realized the difference that this would make. When reflecting on this with my parents, my mom pointed out that Jay's father might not have been present at his birth and, therefore, was not on the birth certificate. Was that something that happened often? I didn't really know. Regardless, my son carries the maternal side of his biological father, and not his paternal side—a connection that I will continue to question and reflect upon throughout life.

Now, in 2018, I view names differently—and Ahmad's name, specifically. I can tell when people question his name, do not understand his name, or do not take the time to pronounce his name correctly. Correctly pronouncing someone's name displays care and overall respect.

As far as Ahmad is concerned, I like to make people feel uncomfortable with the idea of a name. When people are put in an uncomfortable position, they are more likely to remember the situation, the feeling, and the message. I want people to question their idea of a "normal" name in America, which often comes down to the idea of a Eurocentric-sounding name.

Scene Jump Cut: 2012
Husband No. 2

Identity.

Identity comes in many forms. It can come through the form of a name based in family tradition. It can come through family, love, and a choice to be part of one's life and experiences. It can come in the form of genetic testing, which reveals where you "came from" in the wider world.

When my son was 3 years old, I met a man who would become my second husband within a year of meeting on Match.com. Doug was (and still is) a gentle, caring, open-minded, and diligent father and husband. He is our rock. Before we were married or even engaged, Ahmad began calling him "Dougie Dad." I remember the first time vividly.

One overcast Saturday afternoon, Ahmad, my dad, and I were standing in a hallway at church. My dad and I were talking about the schedule for the upcoming week, because he helped out a lot in transporting and watching Ahmad. He was Ahmad's solid father figure, as he had been mine for all the years of my life.

"Okay, Dad. I am going to take him to preschool in the morning on Monday, but can you make sure to pick him up? And then next Saturday is when swim class begins. Will you be around for that?" While my dad was extremely helpful, I also had to remind him about things multiple times; I wanted to make sure he was paying attention each time.

"Yes. I have all of that on my schedule," my dad said, as he looked at his paper calendar.

Impatiently waiting for us to finish our conversation, Ahmad looked up and said, "Can we just go home now so I can see Dad?"

My dad and I froze. We looked at each other, and then down at Ahmad. You could tell from Ahmad's expression that he realized what he had just done and was a little bit embarrassed. However, after the initial shock, my dad and I did not miss a beat.

"Sure, we are leaving. We can go home and see Dougie Daddy," I said. This name stuck with Doug for many years before the adoption, and is still sometimes heard in our house.

In my head, that is the day that Ahmad truly saw Doug as his dad.

After finishing up the schedule conversation with my dad, Ahmad and I walked out to the parking lot to get into my blue Honda Fit and drove the 20 miles to "Dougie Daddy's" house.

When we arrived at Doug's house, Ahmad unbuckled himself from his car seat and waited for me to open his door. Before I could get around to open it, Doug had come out of his house and was opening Ahmad's door.

"Hey, buddy. How's your day going?" Doug asked Ahmad, as they embraced.

"Good. Berkley now?" Ahmad asked. Berkley was Doug's golden retriever.

"Sure. Let's go inside first, and then we can take him for a walk," I said.

When we walked into the house, we were greeted by Berkley. He wagged his huge, fluffy tail, licked us, and jumped up on each of us to show how happy that he was to see us.

After dropping off our things in the bedroom—we were going to be staying the night at Doug's house—we got the leash for Berkley and were off on our walk.

Berkley did this cute thing where he would put the part of the leash closest to him in his mouth, so it looked like he was walking himself, but he would also let Ahmad hold the leash. They walked along together in front of us as Doug and I held hands and talked. It had turned into a beautiful, sunny, fall day.

After going around the block to the park and playing for a little bit, we returned home. Berkley slopped water out of his water bowl, Ahmad got a popsicle and Doug and I each got a glass of water. We talked about what we wanted for dinner and finished off our evening with a movie.

The next morning, Ahmad and I were getting ready to go to church. We packed up our bags from the night before and Doug made us breakfast. We were not yet to the point in our relationship in which Doug came to church with us.

After breakfast, Ahmad and I began walking toward the door. Standing at the door, 3-year-old Ahmad looked up at Doug and said, "Can I have a hug, Dad?"

"Sure, buddy," Doug replied. "But—I'm not your dad."

They hugged, and I put Ahmad in his car seat and shut the door.

I turned around to say goodbye to Doug, but before saying goodbye, I said in a low, but very serious voice: "If he wants to call you 'Dad,' he will call you 'Dad' and you will deal with it." My direct personality was on full display that morning.

Taken aback some, Doug responded, "Okay."

We kissed, and I was off with Ahmad to drive the 20 miles to church.

That day—the day Ahmad first called Doug "Dad"—was the day we all realized that identity does not come from blood or genetics, but from love, caring, and family.

Scene Jump Cut: 2014

After a year of marriage, Doug and I began talking about his adoption of Ahmad. Jay had not followed through with his visitation (or child support) since Ahmad and I moved away from Chicago.

Sitting at the kitchen table in our new house, I turned to Doug and asked, "Would you be willing to adopt Ahmad?"

The kids were not within earshot, and I wanted to have this conversation alone. At this point, at the end of 2013, Ahmad had not seen his father in two years. My father, as a minister, had presided over nine funerals in the span of two weeks, one of which was someone around my age. I realized that if I died, Ahmad's life would be turned upside down—and death is an inevitable part of life.

Hearing the question, Doug turned, with a wet glass and a drying towel in his hands and said, "Umm, what?"

"You know how my dad has had so many funerals lately?" I said hesitantly, as he came to sit with me at the table.

"Yes."

"Well, you know that if something happened to me, God forbid, that Ahmad would have to go back to the Mayfield family—a family he does not know. You know how sensitive he is. That would really mess up his life, to lose his mom and then have to be taken from the only family he knows."

Beginning to understand, Doug said, "Yes. I guess I have never really thought about that. That *would* be awful."

"Well," I said, looking him directly in the eyes, "Would you adopt Ahmad, so we can make sure you are always his dad?"

Doug immediately said, "Yes. Yes. You know I am his dad. This just makes sense."

The next day, Doug contacted the lawyer who had represented him in his divorce from his first wife. We set up a meeting with the lawyer and began the process of adoption.

The meeting with the lawyer took place about a week later. After explaining the situation, she looked at me and said, "You know that you need to at least contact your ex-husband to see if he will agree. If he doesn't, it just makes it a little more difficult."

Swallowing hard, I said, "Okay. I will email him."

We continued our meeting. She told us that Ahmad would be assigned a guardian *ad litem* (GAL) to represent and investigate what was in his best interest. We talked about the process of going to court and she made it very clear that if Doug and I were to get divorced in the future, Ahmad would still be his son. Doug would get rights and pay child support.

Once we left the meeting, I wrote Jay an email:

> *I hope you are doing well.*
>
> *I am emailing to discuss something with you. I have contacted my lawyer here and we are going to be moving forward with my husband, Doug, in the adoption process of Ahmad. When you get served I want you to understand why we are going through with this. We are not changing his name, until or if ever Ahmad wants to, and I will not lose contact with you or your family. However, this is in the best interest of Ahmad. It would be cost-effective and better for everyone if you would consent willingly. You will still be able to have the same relationship you currently do with Ahmad. Ahmad is currently on Doug's health insurance, Doug financially supports Ahmad and me, and he is there every day for him. Upon the consent and adoption we will waive all child support from the past and in the near future. You will be free and clear of all the past child support you have failed to send.*
>
> *Again, I hope we can do this peacefully and I also hope you can see how this is in the best interest for Ahmad, who is building a life with Doug and his little sisters here.*
>
> *Thank you.*

While I would like to report that after that email, the process went smoothly, that would be a lie. By the time we were beginning the adoption process, Jay was living in Wisconsin, which was technically against our divorce agreement (we were both to stay in the state of Illinois). However, with him living in Wisconsin and claiming that he did not have enough money for court or for traveling to court, the process took much longer than expected.

On a date in July, when we all believed that everything would go smoothly and the adoption would be finalized, Ahmad dressed in a brand-new superhero T-shirt—cape and all. Doug had on a suit and borrowed my dad's superhero tie. We were all ready to join together, under one last name.

That morning, my dad, Ahmad, and I arrived at the courthouse. We went through the metal detector and made our way to the second floor. We were waiting in front of the courtroom for our lawyer when I heard my dad say, "Isn't that Jay?"

My stomach sank, my blood pressure went up, and I thought I was going to be sick. I turned around and—yes, it was him. "Yes," I said, my voice quivering.

"It is going to be okay, Anni. Just breathe," my dad said.

I couldn't think straight. He was not getting my son!

I turned back around, and our lawyer was standing there. I looked at her and said, "He is here."

"What? Who? You mean Jay?" she responded, confused.

"Yes," Doug said. "He is sitting over there."

"Okay," the lawyer said. "Well, I am going to go talk to him to see what is going on."

Down the hallway, Jay was sitting on a bench with a woman who had come with him. I assumed that it was the mother of his newest son, who lived in Wisconsin. Our lawyer went over to him, had a conversation, and then came back to us.

"Okay, well, it will be a bit more confusing and involved since he showed up, but we are going to be okay. He does not have representation."

When it was our time to see the judge, the guard called us in. Doug and I entered with our lawyer, Ahmad stayed out on the bench with my dad, and Jay came in with the woman he had arrived with.

Once in the courtroom, Jay said his piece, our lawyer talked, and finally, a court-appointed lawyer was assigned to Jay. During these discussions, I was frantically texting my dad, asking him to take Ahmad and to get him out of the courthouse as quickly as he could. I was in panic mode.

When the court appearance was over, I raced out of the courtroom to make sure that my dad and Ahmad had left. They had not. Ahmad had been playing a game on my dad's phone and as a result, my dad had not received the text messages. I grabbed Ahmad's hand and had one goal: to get out of the courthouse without being stopped by Jay. *Get out of the courthouse. Just get out of the courthouse.* I am sure that people would say that I thought there was some sort of emergency—and in my frantic mind, there was. I had to get my son out of the courthouse. Ahmad was not going to be taken from me by Jay.

We got to our car, buckled up, and pulled away. I breathed a sigh of relief.

"Dammit," I said under my breath, though loud enough for Doug to hear me.

"I know. We are going to be just fine. It will just take a little longer," Doug said calmly.

Several months later, we were back in the courtroom. My mom and dad had both come this time because today was officially going to be "the day." We had settled on a strange agreement in which Doug would adopt Ahmad, but Jay could still see him based around specific and defined meeting dates, points, payments, etc. Jay did not want to show up in court that day, but agreed to "show up" virtually, via FaceTime. The judge asked him questions. My heart was pounding out of my chest. What if Jay did not agree? Then what?

Finally—after what seemed like hours, but I am sure was only a few minutes—the judge turned to where Doug, Ahmad, and I were sitting, next to our lawyer. The judge reiterated the importance of the adoption, the obligations that adopting Ahmad placed on Doug, and verified that this was the path we wanted to take.

Choking back tears, I said, "Judge, I just want to say that we are not doing this to take Ahmad away from his biological father. We are doing this so that if something happens to me, his life does not get turned upside down. We want him to have a relationship with his biological father and will support that relationship the best we can." By this point, I was clawing my legs with my fingernails to try to stop my tears from flowing.

"Thank you for saying that. That makes me feel a lot better, in this situation. I can tell that you have Ahmad's best interest at heart," the judge said, with a smile.

And with that, the papers were signed and Ahmad was officially adopted by Doug! Ahmad was officially a Reinking. Well, a Mayfield-Reinking, but we were all officially a family. And throughout the years I have repeatedly said, "I picked the best daddy for you!" And I truly mean it.

But now, we had to realize that we were two white people raising a socially perceived black boy. What would that mean for our identity? What would that mean for Ahmad's identity?

The challenge to our identity that occurs most frequently centers around the concept of adoption. Most people assume that Doug and I both adopted Ahmad. This angers me beyond measure.

A common conversation in our house (especially when Ahmad was younger) always began with me angrily entering a room where Doug was sitting and saying, "I do not understand why people assume I adopted Ahmad. Look at him. We are identical other than our skin color."

"I know," Doug would say calmly. "I never understand that, either. There is no question that he has your genes."

"Doesn't it make you mad? Don't people at work ask you about it?" I would need constant confirmation from him in the first few months.

"Yeah, but I don't let it get to me all that much, though. Usually, I just say that he is from your first marriage and then we all move on."

"I guess. Maybe it just makes me mad because he is mine and it seems like people don't see that."

"Yeah, people are dumb."

Scene Jump Cut: November 2014
Small-town Illinois

It was time for us to get Ahmad a passport. We had received Ahmad's new birth certificate, with Doug's name on it—which, for me, had been a weird piece of mail to receive. It somehow made it all very surreal.

Knowing we were going to be traveling internationally, we took the birth certificate, the passport photos, and the passport application, and drove to a small town outside of the city where we lived to get a passport, because there, it would be a faster and easier process to get a passport.

Once we got to the post office, Doug, Ahmad, and I got out of the car and walked in.

"Good afternoon. It's chilly out there today, isn't it? How can I help you?" the person behind the desk said with a smile.

"Yeah." I responded in a no-nonsense way, but still showed a smile. "We are here to apply for a passport for him," I said, pointing to Ahmad.

"Oh, okay. Well, we need a lot of paperwork. Are you two his …" she paused for a few seconds, to look from me to Doug and then back to me. "His parents? Like, his real parents?"

Not picking up on the clues, I joyfully responded, "Oh, yeah, he was just adopted by my husband. He is from my first marriage."

"Well, do you have all of the paperwork?" she asked, somewhat shortly.

At this point, Doug was visibly agitated. "Yes, here they are," he said forcefully, as he slid all of the necessary paperwork across the counter.

Looking at him, the postal worker began smiling again, somewhat sensing that she was being too intrusive. "Oh, well, great, honey. We just need you both to sign here." She pointed to two spots on the form and then began looking over Ahmad's new birth certificate—the certificate with Doug's name as his father. "Well, it looks like we are all set. You will just need to pay and we can send it off."

I paid for the passport and the three of us walked outside to get back into our car.

After buckling Ahmad into his seat and closing the door, I looked at Doug and asked, "What's the matter?" We were both still outside of the car, so Ahmad could not hear our conversation.

"You know what she was doing, don't you? She was questioning whether we were family. She was asking too many questions that did not concern her. We had the right paperwork, she was just being nosy." He was getting more and more disconcerted as he was relaying the events back to me. He grew up in this town and he was sensitive to the nosy nature of the community members.

"Oh, my gosh, I didn't even realize that," I said. "God damn, I am pissed now!" My tone got harsher. "What can we do?"

"Nothing. What do you want to do?"

"I guess nothing. Okay." With that, Doug and I got into the car and began our 20-minute drive home.

In that same month—the month of the passport incident—Doug had a friend post an article on Facebook that was titled: *Grace in a Trader Joe's parking lot: This act of kindness changed one mother's life.* It was an article posted on Today.com. In the article, the author describes an incident in which a white woman, in a Trader Joe's store, was stopped by a clerk. The white mother had her adopted African-American children with her. As the article stated:

> *"Ma'am!" I stopped and turned to find a young woman rushing toward me. A bright smile covered her face and I immediately noticed her beautiful black curls, just like the black curls snuggled on my chest, tickling my chin. Recognizing her shirt, I realized that she worked there and assumed I must have dropped something. I looked at her, holding back my tears, waiting.*

> *"I just wanted you to have this bouquet ..." and I looked down to see the flowers in her hands. She quickly continued to explain.*

> *"I was adopted as a baby and it has been a wonderful thing. We need more families like yours." I stared at her, stunned. Hadn't she seen what a disaster we were in the store? Didn't she see that we were barely able to keep it together? Didn't she see what I felt were all my failures as a mom?*

While many people saw this as an act of grace or an act of kindness, I saw the story from a different lens—and so did Doug. After reading the article, he posted on his friend's wall, who had shared the article.

> *Doug: "So ... because the kids have different skin color than the people they're with at the store, they must be adopted?"*
>
> *Friend 1: "Well, Doug, when you have two black children screaming 'Mom' and 'Dad' to two white parents, I think you can assume that at least one of these white folks is not the biological parent, right?"*
>
> *Random comment from another user: "What a neat story. We should do this more often, even with the mothers who didn't adopt their children but are going through the everyday stress that mothers often have to go through."*
>
> *Doug: "I didn't see in the article that the kids were screaming 'Mom' and 'Dad.'"*
>
> *Doug: "I read a different article recently, about a family shopping at Wal-Mart. A white husband was taking his screaming, biracial children out of the store and some shoppers called the cops on him because they thought he was kidnapping them."*
>
> *Friend 1: "Really, Doug? I think you're missing the point of the article and you woke up super sensitive this morning. In your case, if someone ran up to you and Anni, the lady would be right—you did adopt Ahmad. So what is the problem—not down with appreciation to adoptive parents? Go back to bed."*
>
> *Doug: "I get the point of the article. In this lady's case, it turned her day around to have someone acknowledge her frustration and appreciate that she chose to adopt. But if that employee made the same comment to Anni, it would have had the opposite effect and pissed her off, since Ahmad isn't adopted. I guess what I'm saying is it's all about perspective. In this story, the employee assumed correctly. If this happened to my family, then she assumed wrong."*

Scene Jump Cut: 2016
Parents' house

While there have been many experiences in which adoption, skin color, and questioning have arisen in our lives, one stands out. In 2016, we were sitting at my parents' kitchen table with missionaries from Kenya. Our church was sponsoring these missionaries. When I returned from Kenya, my father's church opened and continues to sponsor an orphanage for boys, since the street boys I met when I was there had nowhere to sleep at night. A Kenyan man, his Norwegian wife, and their young daughter were running the orphanage.

There were a total of eight of us sitting around the kitchen table: the missionaries and their daughter, my parents, and my family. We began eating the meal my mother had cooked: hamburgers, hot dogs, and baked beans—a true Midwest meal.

"So, when did you go to Kenya?" the woman asked.

"I was there in 2006. I lived in Nairobi for a bit and then moved to Mombasa," I said.

She continued the questioning. "When was your son born?"

"He is 7, so he was born in 2009."

I smiled as I responded, but I could sense my husband getting more and more uncomfortable next to me. His face is quite telling, and he is not good at hiding what he is thinking. "I was living in Chicago when I had him," I continued.

"Oh, and when did you come back from Kenya?"

Not realizing that this round of questioning was anything other than her trying to get to know me, I responded jovially, "I got back in 2006. I came back around Christmastime."

At this point in the conversation, my mother began asking about their trip and how their daughter, who was quite young, did on the plane rides. Dinner and small talk continued, and eventually, my family left to go home.

When we got in the car, shut the doors, and turned on the ignition, my husband immediately turned to me and said, "You know what they were doing, don't you?"

Caught a little off-guard, I said, "What? What are you talking about?"

"When she was asking you about Ahmad. She was asking you about all of those dates. She was trying to figure out if you'd had him in Kenya, or if he had a Kenyan dad. Like you were lying about where he was born."

"Oh my gosh," I said, stunned, "I didn't even realize that. I thought it was just small talk. But I can totally see that now. How did I miss that?"

"That is why I was getting so agitated," he said. "Why would you lie about it? Why would she question you like that?" He began to speak faster.

"I don't know. That sucks. But, whatever," I said. "It is over now. He is mine and he is not Kenyan, so she can question me all she wants."

After that, we drove home, pulled into our garage, and went inside to put our son to bed.

Identity is family and love—and only sometimes genetics.

Scene Jump Cut: 2017
Second grade, Ahmad

The adoption finalized when Ahmad was in kindergarten and showed us, as a family, that identity means family; it means a name; and it means love. However, in second grade, Ahmad began asking about his "other family." I am friends via Facebook with many family members from Jay's side of Ahmad's biological family, and we would speak occasionally. Nevertheless, Ahmad still wanted to know more about himself.

Years earlier, my mom had bought my dad a *National Geographic* genetic testing kit. So, I thought that a genetic testing kit might be an interesting way for Ahmad to "see" who he is and where he came from. 23andMe was a popular brand at this time, so I purchased it and waited for it to arrive.

The day came in the mail, I don't know who was more excited—Ahmad or me. I explained to him what he had to do. He basically had to spit into a small tub, and then I would seal it up. We would send it back to the company and, in a few weeks, we would know where his ancestors had come from.

"That is awesome, Mom. When we get it back, can I take it to school? We are talking about ancestry now and I think this would be cool to talk about in class," Ahmad said excitedly, in between spits into the tub (he had a lot to fill up!).

"Sure, buddy. We can send it in to school if you would like." I was concentrating on not spilling his spit and following the directions on the package. After sealing it and sending it off, I was able to follow its progress on the computer.

About six weeks after I sent in the sample, I received an email notification that Ahmad's genetic report was ready. I waited for Ahmad to come home from school and we both sat down in front of my computer to read about his genetics.

Most of the ancestry was what we expected—almost 60 percent was from European-like countries—because both of my parents had completed the test previously. Then we began to look at the other portion of his genetics. He had little pockets around the world, with a majority of the remaining amount being in Western Africa.

"Why do you think that is, Mom?" Ahmad asked, inquisitively.

Always being honest with my son, I said, "Well, most of the slaves were from Western African countries when they were taken and sold in America. I would assume you might have some slaves in your family on your biological father's side."

"Really? That is weird. But, I guess that makes sense, right?" He turned to me to either affirm or deny his assumption.

"Yeah. Not all, but a lot of black people in America have a history of being slaves in their family ancestry."

Since completing this DNA test, I have heard more and more about the science behind the process. While it is important and interesting to find out ancestry, the science is not yet perfect—especially for people of color. Regardless of the exactness of his results, it still is interesting that since receiving his genetics, Ahmad has been more and more interested in traveling to and visiting Ghana, one of the West African countries depicted in his genetic map. Maybe one day, when he steps on the soil of his faraway ancestors, he will feel a connection … a connection to another form of his identity.

Blog post: September 12, 2018
Do You Want to Meet Him?

Sitting at the dining room table eating dinner Ahmad said, "We talked about sad stuff today at school. Some people had some real sad stories."

Both Doug and I looked at each other quizzically and then looked back at Ahmad. "Oh, why?"

"It was SEL time, Mom. You know, social emotional."

"Oh yes, of course. Did you share anything?" I asked.

"Yeah. Mine was not as sad as everyone else. Like they had people die."

"Oh. Okay. Well what did you share?"

"Oh, you know. Like Jay stuff. Like how you guys got divorced and I don't see him."

Knowing teachers, because I was one of those teachers who liked to asked lots of questions, I asked, "Oh, did your teacher ask you any questions?"

"Yeah, she just asked if I ever saw him and I said no, not since I was 2."

"Oh okay. Do you want to talk about it more?"

"No."

Our dinner continued with talking about our day. However, that night, the next day, and a few days after I replayed that conversation in my head over and over again.

A few days later, when Ahmad and I were alone in the car, I flat out asked him if he had any desire to see or meet his biological dad, Jay.

"You know I would take you to meet him if you wanted to."

"Yeah, I know Mom. I don't want to meet him."

Somewhat surprised I said, "Okay, I just thought since you talked about it the other day you might want to. I have been thinking about it and wanted to make sure you knew that you could always meet him."

"Yeah, mom, I know. You tell me that all the time. Do you know who I do want to meet?"

"Who?"

"My siblings."

"Huh," I said taking a deep breath, "Well, that is going to be a little bit harder. I know you have at least three. One lives in Croatia, one lives in Chicago, but I don't know anything about her, and then you have a little brother in Wisconsin. To me honest, I don't know if you have any other brothers or sisters. Maybe when you get a little older we can meet your older sister overseas."

"Yeah. I knew it would be hard. I don't want to meet Jay, but I do want to meet my siblings sometime."

The conversation ended there with more questions circling around in my head.

Kids' minds are curious. Kids' minds are mysterious. Ahmad does not share any of Doug's genes, however he is his dad. He cleans up his vomit. He takes him to superhero movies. He shares a love of Weird Al. He is everything Ahmad needs in a father and role model.

Ahmad has no desire to meet a man that walked out of his life, even if they share genes. Who does he want to meet? The individuals in his generation that share his genes. He does not have any half or full siblings on my side. So, I can understand his need to make a connection to individuals who share genes. One day that connection will be made. However, right now, I can only offer him to meet a man who Ahmad does not view as family, or his extended family. But honestly, I hope someday he does ask to meet Jay. Why? I am not sure. But I feel like at some point in his life it would be important. But am I going to push it? No.

As families continue to diversify through marriage, adoption, foster care, blended families, divorce, or any other combination of family dynamics, what "family" means continually expands and evolves. Family is an identity and identity is not stagnant.

8

Hair

"Having your dad cut your hair is a rite of passage for black folk."

Ear Hustle podcast, 2018

"I didn't even know we had a hair chart."

**The Stoop podcast, 2018 (Referring to the
Andre Walker Hair Typing System)**

*"Black hair has its beginnings in incredibly tough circumstances. Taken to foreign lands
and forced to submit to European standards of beauty, we've had incredible strain
placed upon our hair to look and behave a certain way. The varied styles that have
evolved have seen a return of more natural textures with a nod to the versatility that the
choice is ours now and ours alone. But some struggles with this topic still remain."*

Fashion writer, Kristin Booker, 2014

*"If you're white and have a black child placed with you (adoption or foster
care), for the love of God, get some help with their skin and hair."*

The Moth podcast (referring to transracial adoption)

Scene Jump Cut: 2011
Peoria, Illinois

One of the first things Ahmad recognized as "different" between himself and me was his hair. Hair intrigues him, especially the way it looks and feels. So, on one morning when he was just a toddler, he was in the stage of regularly referring to people's hair.

"Hey, Mommy, look—that man looks like me!"

Three-year-old Ahmad had excitedly yelled out while we were on a walk in our neighborhood, which was a regular after-dinner activity of ours since having moved closer to my parents and out of Chicago. Ahmad was a little ways ahead of me and was pointing to an African-American man who was taking out garbage across the street. I sheepishly smiled and did the Midwestern-type wave to the gentleman as I bowed my head. Under my breath, I said, "Shhh, yes, honey, he does."

Being only 3 years old, Ahmad did not understand that I was trying to tell him to be quiet. So, he continued—and quite loudly. "Like, his hair—it's just like mine! I am like him."

By this point, we had turned the corner. I think we were out of ear-shot of the man who was taking out his garbage. I turned to Ahmad and smiled, "Oh, yes, you are right. You both have the same texture hair." Ahmad was pointing out his hair. Sometimes children tell the truth in their own unique ways.

We continued down the street, and in just a few more steps, we were at our driveway. We had a steep driveway, so we both started the climb upward. I opened the one-car garage door with the opener I had taken with us on the walk. It was a humid night and we both were a little parched, so when we got inside, I walked to the refrigerator and got two popsicles out of the freezer. I opened Ahmad's and then I opened mine. We sat on the couch, side by side, eating our popsicles and cooling off before bath time.

Before bath time, however, Ahmad finished his popsicle and, with a sticky toddler hand, reached over and touched my hair. My hair reached just past my shoulders, and was thin and dark blonde in color.

"Mommy, I like your hair," Ahmad said soothingly, as he tried to run his sticky fingers through my hair.

"I like yours, too, honey," I said, "My hair is brown. What color is your hair?"

"Dark."

And with that, it was time for his bath.

Ah, hair.

Since Ahmad was little, his fascination with hair has been undeniable. His biological father had hip long dreadlocks, so even as an infant, he would pull on the ends of Jay's hair and put them in his mouth. (Yes, I know—a little gross, but it was comforting to Ahmad.) When Ahmad and I moved away from Chicago, the thing I missed most was having someone to help me figure out how to take care of Ahmad's hair. I was knowledgeable enough to know that I did not understand the ins and outs of taking care of coarser hair, so I sought out barbers in our new town.

Since finding a great barber for Ahmad, I have also begun to recognize the deeper, institutional differences between white people's hair and black people's hair. With a little assistance and guidance from a podcast I recently listened to, I came to realize that "everyone" knows how to deal with "white" hair, because products are marketed to white people. Commercials describe "white" hair; movies, television shows, and other types of media consumed by the wider public describe how to care for and do "white" hair. But how many mainstream books, television shows, movies, or other types of media describe how to take care of black people's hair? Essentially, they are few and far between, and are often not consumed by the wider public. Does everyone have the same knowledge of taking care of black people's hair? No. That realization has come with some huge mistakes on my part.

Scene Jump Cut: 2010
Barber shopping

Both of my parents grew up in the town Ahmad and I moved to after my divorce. My parents left this specific town for about 20 years, to raise my sister and me in Iowa, but moved back when my father's parents were ailing. When Ahmad and I decided to move close to my parents (mainly for help, as I was a single mother) I reached out to my dad to see if he could find a barber for Ahmad—a barber who knew how to do black people's hair. I asked my dad because he was essentially going to take over the paternal role in Ahmad's life, and honestly, I was uncomfortable going into a black barbershop. My father, on the other hand, had no hesitations.

My father began researching barbershops by asking around and driving through town. He finally found a barbershop that was reputable and was willing to let a white man sit in their barbershop during peak hours. (Yes, some barbershops basically said, "Nah, you can't come in here then. They might think you are the cops.") My dad also had some stipulations that not every barber was willing to agree to: show up when I have an appointment, and keep my time open if we agree to it. The man my father found to cut Ahmad's hair was a veteran barber, who over the years has found my dad to be a great person to talk to during Ahmad's haircuts.

So, one Saturday morning, my dad picked up Ahmad and they were off to their first barbershop appointment. Since that first time, my dad and Ahmad have had the bonding experience of going to a black barbershop, getting Ahmad's hair cut, and building memories that will last a lifetime. Since finding Ahmad's go-to barber, they have built a relationship: my dad, the barber, and Ahmad. Ahmad is also getting the experience of entering, listening to, and being part of the culture in a black barbershop—something that I believe is important to his growth, as a black boy in America.

In the years I was with Jay, I would often hear him talk about barbershops and the life lessons he learned in that setting. He described the experiences almost as a rite of passage, and I was not going to deny my son of that just because Jay was an absent father. I knew that barbershops—and the conversations and experiences in those barbershops—were a rite of passage; a foundation of black male identity; a developed sense of community and camaraderie. I knew that Ahmad would gain something from the barbershop.

Ahmad did gain information from the barbershop: He learned of varying life circumstances, and he learned about the negative views men in the barbershop held about males showing any feminine qualities. In my view, he learned both positive and negative mindsets. The experiences and conversations he hears also result in questions, conversations, and at times, him growing up a little faster than I had expected. Aside from the conversations and chatter in the barbershop, along with the bootlegged movies constantly playing, three events have particularly stuck out to Ahmad and my dad over the years.

The first event occurred in 2013, when young men in our city were hired by a new bookie in town to "square up" with people who owed money to the bookie he took over for. One of the young men hired to "scare" (break in, rob, etc.) people into paying what was owed was the son of Ahmad's barber. The son was in his late teens and was convicted of invasion, along with other, more serious charges. He was sentenced to many years in prison.

This story is important because my dad has the tendency to get to know people, talk to people, and relate to people. So, after the robberies and home invasions, Dad found out that the barber's son was on trial for the home invasions, as were many other young, black men in the community.

The other men involved in the crimes talked; the barber's son did not, and therefore, he did not get a plea bargain. He was sentenced to many years—so many years, in fact, that he will probably never see the outside of a prison again.

Since the time of his son's arrest, the barber has always updated Dad on his family happenings. My dad has sent letters to the barber's son, in prison, as a way to connect him to the outside world. The barber will tell my dad—and consequently, Ahmad—about visiting his son. While Ahmad is quite good at *pretending* not to listen, he overhears a lot.

One late morning, Dad pulled into my driveway to drop off Ahmad after a haircut. I unlocked and opened the door.

With a giant smile, I said, "Hey, Ahmad! How was the barber today? I love your haircut!"

He walked past me into the house, and said, "It was fine. Nothing interesting."

Still curious—because I know they always talk about something—I continued my line of questioning. "Did the barber talk to you at all?"

By this time, Dad had walked into the house behind him, laid some of Ahmad's belongings on the table right inside the door, gave me a kiss on the forehead, and was off. He was on his way to a funeral. "Bye, Dad."

Ahmad went to go sit on the couch and play video games. He answered my earlier question with, "No, he just talked to Pop about his son."

"Oh, what did you hear?" (Honestly, I liked to hear the gossip.)

"Well, he just got out of the SHU. He was just talking to Pop about that," Ahmad said nonchalantly. By this time, the video game console was on and I knew that I was going to lose him to *Madden NFL* any minute now.

A little surprised, I said, "Oh. Do you know what the SHU is?"

Ahmad turned to me while his gaming system was loading and said, "Yeah, I asked Pop. It is where he has to go be by himself because he did something bad. I think I heard he got into a fight." Again, Ahmad was saying these statements very factually.

"Oh, well, cool. Your haircut is awesome, it's just what you wanted." The conversation dwindled off as Ahmad began playing *Madden NFL*.

Another time, Dad brought Ahmad into the house in the late morning, just as he always does after a haircut appointment. This time, though, he seemed more distant than usual.

I smiled at them both and said, "Hey guys, how was the barber today? Ahmad, I like your hair." I was in the middle of carrying laundry up the stairs, but I happily put it down to talk to Dad and Ahmad.

"Good," Ahmad said, and walked into the living room to watch TV with his sisters, leaving my dad and me in the foyer.

"Something happened today at the barber. It was queer," my dad said, turning to face me. (My dad uses the word "queer" to mean "odd." I have told him multiple times that using that word in that way is actually not politically correct, but he is set in his ways.)

"Oh, really? What?" My mind was racing. It could be anything.

My dad continued, "Well, there was a boy there—an African-American boy—who was sweeping the floors. He was probably junior high-age. I asked him how school was going, and he said that he was expelled for the rest of the year. Then he said that he was there, working for his dad, to keep busy and earn some money, since he couldn't go to school right now."

Interrupting my dad, I said, "Oh, that sucks."

"Yeah. Well, after he was done talking to me, he kept sweeping and his dad pulled him aside. He was getting in trouble for talking to me—sharing his business with a white man. I could hear what the man was saying to his son. When I saw this happen, I turned to Ahmad's barber and said, 'That is racism, you know.' Telling his son not to trust the white man; don't tell the white man your business; that is as much racism as going the other way." I could tell that my dad was in a state of reflection after this encounter.

"Oh! Did the other barber hear you? What did Ahmad's barber say?"

"No, the guy yelling at his kid didn't hear me. And Ahmad's barber agreed. He said that he never thought of it that way, but that I was right. I just felt bad for the kid. I didn't say this to him, but as I was driving home, I was thinking about how deep-seated it is—it comes from the times of slavery, it seems like, when slaves did not want to share anything with their owners because their owners were not to be trusted," my dad said in a state of reflection. He continued, saying, "I didn't say this to him, either, but racism cuts both ways. Being fearful and suspicious of white people, out of self-preservation, is still racist."

"Yeah, I can see that. That is unfortunate," I said. I didn't know what else to say. With that, we said our goodbyes and he was out the door. I was still thinking about that interaction, thinking about what he had said. I was thinking about racism. I was thinking about what Ahmad might have picked up—if anything—from the interactions of that day. I never asked him.

One last experience impacted Ahmad more than it influenced my dad. When Ahmad was younger, he enjoyed wearing one of my old scarfs as his winter scarf. One in particular that was soft, vibrant lime-green, and "looked" feminine. I am the type of parent who doesn't care what a child wears as long as he or she is comfortable and not breaking any laws. So, he wore that lime green-scarf for an entire winter season.

On this specific day, I picked Ahmad up from preschool and was taking him to my dad's house, so they could go get his hair cut before school pictures later in the week. I pulled into my dad's driveway, unlocked the doors, and Ahmad and I got out of the car. We walked up the small path to the front door and my dad was there to greet us.

"Hello!" he said. "How was school Ahmad? Are you ready for your haircut?"

Ahmad smiled back at him and said, "Good, yes."

My dad looked down at Ahmad and said, "Are you going to wear that to the barbershop?" He was referring to Ahmad's scarf.

I whipped my head around to my dad and gave him a dirty look. "Yes, why?" I responded for Ahmad.

"Well, don't you think it looks a little girly?" He could tell that he was going to get in trouble with me.

"What is girly, Dad? Ahmad is wearing it, so, no—it is not girly," I said, obviously becoming and more and more agitated.

Ahmad, paying close attention, looked up at Dad and said, "Can I wear it?"

My father nodded his head, looked at me, and then guided Ahmad to his car. I waved to them as they left and went inside my parents' house to wait for them to return. I turned on the television and sat on their leather couch.

About an hour later, my dad and Ahmad pulled back into the driveway. I did not hear them pull in, but I heard them when they opened the front door and Ahmad yelled, "Hi, Mom!"

I got up from the couch and walked to the front door. I saw Ahmad standing there with a new haircut—but the scarf was missing. "Where is your scarf, Ahmad?" I was livid. I thought my dad had told him to take it off after they had left the house before the haircut.

"I took it off because the guys were making fun of it," he said.

"Oh, that sucks. I am sorry. They don't know what they are talking about. You looked great in it and can wear it wherever you want." I smiled at him, rubbed his head and told him that he could go watch television. He ran to the back room, where the television was playing, and I waited for my dad at the door.

When he walked up the front path and was close enough to hear me, I said, "What happened with the scarf?" I was not mad, but actually rather sad for Ahmad.

My dad stepped inside the house as I held open the front door, and said, "Well, the guys in the barbershop were kind of making fun of it, so Ahmad took it off. They didn't say anything to him, but you could hear them talking."

"And you didn't say anything?" I asked.

"No. Ahmad just handed me the scarf and we moved on with the haircut. I know, I know. I should have said something." He was apologetic.

"Okay, as long as you get it. Ahmad can wear whatever he wants, and we will support him." I was matter-of-fact.

I walked into the back room to sit with Ahmad and watch television with him, before we left and headed back to our house.

Many years ago, when my dad first began taking Ahmad to the barbershop, he bought Ahmad a book: *Bippity Bop Barbershop*, by Natasha Anastasia Tarpley. In *Bippity Bop Barbershop*, a young boy named Miles takes his first trip to the barbershop with his father. Both are black males. While Miles is scared at first, his father helps him become more comfortable in the barbershop, pick out a hairstyle, and display bravery when sitting in the barber's chair.

The book is beautiful and is written in a musically jazzy rhythm. It also celebrates African-American identity and shows a positive image of black experiences. For Ahmad, however, the celebration is sometimes overshadowed by the fact that his skin places him in the barbershop community but his cultural knowledge does not.

The message and the "jazziness" of the book has helped Ahmad understand the experience. However, the book has also highlighted the fact that Ahmad does not and will not experience the barbershop with his biological father, a black man who also grew up in a barbershop and understands the community that is built inside the four walls. Rather, Ahmad is experiencing the barbershop with his white maternal grandfather, a man who is open to reflection but does not understand the cultural, deep-seated meaning of a barbershop community.

When I began writing this book, I asked my dad how he felt taking Ahmad to the barbershop, all these years.

He initially said, "I am proud of my grandson." While the answer about Ahmad was simple enough, he did go on to say, "But, I think that sometimes the people in the barbershop are a little hesitant when I am in there. I always make sure to let the barber know I am coming in with Ahmad. There is a perception there. I don't know if it mine, that I am projecting, or if it is really there."

Although Ahmad and my father have found a great barber, I continually have questions. When Ahmad was little, I had so many questions about his hair; when he began growing his hair, I had questions about how often he needed to be lined up and about the process of taking care of it. (Lined up defined: the forehead, temples, and back are shaved into straight lines and sharp angles.) How often should we treat his hair? Which products should we use?

Throughout the years I have been fortunate enough to have people to ask (in addition to his barber), but asking often puts you in a vulnerable spot. When he was little, I reached out to my ex-boyfriend from high school. He is also biracial and I knew he used something specific in his hair when we dated because I remember loving the smell of it. So, randomly—on Facebook one day—I reached out and asked him what he used to put in his hair in high school. The answer: pink lotion. That day, I went out and got a bottle of pink lotion. We still use it to this day, as we do with many other products. Through trial and error we have tried many things, but in all honesty, we have not found "Ahmad's product" yet.

The mistakes of a white mother navigating the process of taking care of her black son's hair came to a peak in 2014. We began to notice that Ahmad was getting lots of dry spots on his head. We usually could see them after his haircut, but I could feel them between barbershop visits. I thought it might be ringworm, or maybe something else that I didn't know about—maybe I was washing his hair too much and it was making it dry? As we later found out, it was a fungus.

Scene Jump Cut: 2014
White mother mistakes

Before going to the doctor and nearly a year after noticing the spots, I was sitting in my living room one night after putting Ahmad to bed. I knew I was doing something wrong, but I didn't know whom to ask. Finally, after scrolling through Facebook and wracking my brain, I thought of someone!

There was a woman I had worked with when I was a teacher in East Chicago, Indiana. She is African-American, has four boys, and was my "go-to" pseudo-mama when Ahmad was an infant and toddler. She was a matriarch—a motherly figure—and would tell you exactly how things were (without caring how she came across) because, "Honey, you need to know how to care for your baby."

So, late one July night, I sent her a message:

Mama Mac—I hope everything is good with you and your family. I have an odd question about Ahmad's hair, and you always gave me good advice when we worked together, so I thought I would give it a try and ask: When he goes to the barber and gets it lined up and cut, he always has one patch of dry skin. Could I be washing his hair too much? Is there something I am supposed to be putting on his hair every day? His hair is pretty coarse, I just don't know if I am doing it right, and his barber is no help. Thanks in advance.

Much later that night, I got a response:

I'm honored you thought of me. Washing too much is very possible. How often? And are you applying an oil or hair lotion after?

It would be much easier if you sent me a pic of the dry area and we can discuss how the barber is cutting his hair as well. I love, love being there for you! We can come up with a plan that works for his grade of hair. My husband can be a big help, so tomorrow after he gets off work I'll catch him up. Love!

My response:

Okay, I will take a picture tomorrow and I didn't know I was supposed to be putting anything on it (lotion, oil), so I haven't been. We wash it like every other day. It looks flaky. At first I thought it was ringworm, but it's not (I took him to the doctor) and he has had the dry scalp for like nine months (we ended up taking him again, to another doctor, and found out it was a fungus), but it's patchy, and not all over. The texture of his hair is so coarse that it is practically water resistant.

She responded back immediately:

Oh no, immediately stop washing his hair that often and tomorrow, take a dime-size amount of olive oil and massage it into his scalp every morning to get the moisture back healthily. It's not ringworm, it's a very dry scalp. Wash his hair once a week or week and a half during the winter. Right now go a full seven days without washing; his hair isn't dirty. The right level of moisture is key to his hair and skin care. You're such a good mom!

Later that week I ended up sending Mama Mac a picture, and the conversation continued for a few more exchanges. That exchange—reaching out to someone I trusted but had not communicated with in years—put me in a place of vulnerability. What if she would have ignored my plea for help or responded in a way that discouraged me? Vulnerability is hard, but when help is needed—especially for your children—it is an obstacle to overcome.

My experience with hair has become a great sense of stress since becoming a mother. What does hair mean? Is hair how we relate to each other? Or is hair where our differences become even wider?

When I was scrolling through Facebook one evening, I saw a picture that many readers probably remember. It was a picture of President Obama bending at the waist, lowering his head so that a young black boy could touch his hair. The boy had asked the president, before the picture was taken, if his hair was like his. The little boy related not to the president's skin color, but to the texture of his hair—something that is tangible. In my experience, children relate to others in many ways, and for some it is through the touch of hair.

What I have learned is that hair has history. Hair allows for expression, but the differences of hair texture and style strikes a harsh reality when people lose jobs or are suspended from school because of their expression through hair. Yes, hair can cost a black person their job. This realization goes back to the discussion about owning one's body and who has control. Who has control of a body when a natural hairstyle can cost someone their job?

9

Skin Color

"You've got to be carefully taught.
You've got to be taught
To be afraid of people
Whose eyes are oddly made
And people whose skin is a different shade
You've got to be carefully taught."

South Pacific

"Infants begin to notice and respond to skin color cues at around 6 months."
Derman-Sparks

If a child is old enough to make fun of another child for being black or brown or for
having dark skin, that child is old enough to learn about racism and colourism.

Shanice Nicole, Black feminist, spoken word artist, and educator

Scene Jump Cut: 2013
Zoo, Peoria, Illinois

"What color is your skin, Jack?"

Ahmad asked his cousin that question while they were sitting on a wooden bench under a maple tree at the zoo. They were sitting on the bench after having looked at the African animals: giraffes, rhinos, zebras, and lions. It was over 100 degrees outside and they needed to cool off, so they were drinking bug juice that Mimi (my mom) had bought them.

Jack and Ahmad were born three years apart, and at the time of this conversation, Ahmad was about 4 years old. When Jack heard that question, he turned to Ahmad and then to Mimi. Mimi responded for him and said, "I would say that Jack has peach skin." Jack, my sister's son, has blonde hair and blue eyes.

Accepting that answer, Ahmad continued. "Mimi, what color is my skin?"

Mimi looked down at his arm and said, "Well, I would say that yours is brown. What do you think?"

Ahmad nodded in agreement and asked one more question. "Mimi, what color is your skin?"

Looking down at her own arm, she said, "Well, I think that I would call my skin polka-dotted." She smiled down at Ahmad, adding, "I have been out in the sun a long time in my life and when people that have my ancestry, German, get to be my age, their skin begins to look a little like mine—with brown and white and pink and black polka dots."

Pleased with the answer, Ahmad said, "Okay. Well, I am cooled off, can we go to the monkeys?"

After walking around the zoo for a little while longer, Ahmad, Jack, and Mimi returned to Mimi's house, for dinner. When they all got home from the zoo, Pop (my dad) was home, sitting on the back porch in his chair and reading a book. Ahmad slid the screen door that led out to the back porch and marched up to Pop with confidence.

"Hey, Pop," Ahmad said as he held his forearm up to Pop's forearm. "Look, we have the same color skin!" Ahmad looked up at Pop and smiled.

My father had been outside in the sun most of the day (and summer) and just like *my* Pop, (Ahmad's great-grandfather) my father's skin was getting darker as he got older. So, when Ahmad held up his arm next to Pop's arm, their forearms were very close to the same shade of brown.

"Yes, you are right. We are the same color today," Pop said with a smile, as he looked at Ahmad and at both of their arms.

From a young age, Ahmad recognized that he had "beautiful brown skin," as he would describe it; he would also inform me that my skin was very "pale and white." However, sometimes I would need to help others understand the logistics of his skin color, and not just fight judgment and prejudice.

When Ahmad was an infant, I would drop him off at Ms. Reese's house during the day. Although she had raised all of the children of the neighborhood over the years, Ahmad was the first biracial baby she had watched. Every summer, I would kindly remind her on a daily basis that Ahmad needed sunscreen on his skin.

"Oh, Ms. Anni, that baby doesn't need that," she would say.

"Ms. Reese, okay, but please put it on him—for me?" I would say, as nicely as I could, even though this conversation occurred daily. I did not want to make her upset because she took amazing care of Ahmad and loved him as her own, but I needed her to understand the importance of sunscreen on his skin.

Standing her ground, Ms. Reese would respond, "This baby will be just fine. He has dark skin, Miss; he is no problem. You just don't worry about it."

Although we never agreed on this topic, I would still show her, every summer, how to put sunscreen on his skin. We would sit in her crowded living room and Ahmad would lie on my lap or on the couch. I would squirt a dime-size amount of sunscreen onto the center of my palm and rub my hands together. Then, I would slowly apply the sunscreen all over Ahmad's body. However, knowing how stubborn Ms. Reese was, I eventually just began putting the sunscreen on Ahmad in the morning, before arriving at her house, and crossing my fingers that its protection would last the entire day.

While interviewing family members for this book, I realized that skin color and race have always been somehow incorporated into our lives. This was surprising to me because, statistically, white families that have been in the United States for many generations benefit from a natural privilege, which usually results in an absent eye to race in America.

When discussing skin color and race with my mother, she clearly recalled that as a child, she was afraid to touch the skin of black children at the city pool because she was afraid it would rub off on her. A decade later, however—when she was a student at the University of Illinois—she ended up with a black roommate for six weeks. While the university did not, at the time, typically place students of two different races in the same dorm room, there were extenuating circumstances that resulted in a six-week amendment to the procedures. Although my mother and her temporary roommate did not grow close in those six weeks, they did have a conversation one night.

Sitting on their respective beds, the roommate said, "I can't tell my grandma that I have a white roommate."

My mom looked up from what she was studying and nodded. "Yeah, I can't tell my grandma, either. My grandma raised my dad to know 'good blacks' and 'bad blacks,' but to her, black people and white people should never socialize."

After my mom relayed these experiences to me, I got the courage to ask her another question. "What do you think about having a black grandson?"

By this point, we were both sitting at her dining room table. We were each playing Solitaire with our own decks of cards, hers red and mine black. When I asked her this question, she stopped playing and made eye contact with me.

"When you first had Ahmad, you still looked very young. I am sure some people thought you were a teenage mom," she said. "When we would go out to stores, I always noticed different reactions from white women and black women. The white women would look to you, to me, and then to Ahmad. The white women would then get a look on their face. It was always the same look, and I couldn't quite figure it out at first. I initially thought, Ahmad is a beautiful baby; I bet they are admiring his long eyelashes and beautiful skin. But then I started to look deeper. They were giving me a look of pity because they thought I had a teenage daughter who'd had a child with a black man. The black women, though, had a completely different reaction. When they saw him in stores with us they would walk right up to him, coo in his face, and comment on how beautiful he was."

As she finished, we both looked back down at our cards and began playing our separate games again. I nodded slightly.

"There was another time when race really came up," she continued, still playing cards. "When you first moved back to be closer to us, I would take Ahmad to soccer practice. I was always nervous because soccer practice was in a part of town where not many black people were even seen. In my head, I was thinking, What would I say if someone said something mean to my grandson? Or about him, while I was sitting in the stands? I would not know what to say. I realized then that I needed to figure out how to stand up and advocate for him."

The place my mother was talking about, where she used to take Ahmad for soccer practice, was in a neighboring town that still had sundown laws in affect in the 1980s. Sundown laws were laws that legally separated cities and villages based on skin color. These laws were always passed by the oppressing group—the white people. Essentially, anyone who had dark skin had to be inside for the day by sundown. While the laws in this area were taken off the books in the 1980s, the mindset is still entrenched in many families and communities. Some comments from more recent events in this specific part of Illinois include the following:

> *In 2006, as reported in the Peoria Journal Star newspaper, a student from the town said to a student from Peoria Manual, a predominately black high school: "Go back across the river, n*****!"*

> *"We have friends who live in town, and they don't want us to drive through alone. We were over there, and it got dark, and they followed us out of town to make sure nothing happened to us."*

> **A black resident, in 2004**

While I was interviewing my dad in the process of writing this book, I asked him about the influence of skin color in his life. While he mentioned that his parents often viewed themselves as members of an oppressed group, due to their level of poverty—and therefore somewhat related to other oppressed groups, such as people of color—he reflected more on his life as a parent.

"Do you remember when we moved?" my dad asked, in response to my question about skin color.

"Yes, I was in fifth grade. I remember helping you guys stuff the envelopes with your resumes and send them off all over the place," I said, recalling my parents applying to co-minister positions.

My dad and I were riding in his car to a 5K we were going to run together, in a tradition that began after Ahmad's birth. I was in the passenger seat and he was driving. The air was blasting and it was 6 a.m., and with a long drive ahead of us, I knew we would have time to have this conversation.

My dad continued. "Well, do you remember the day I took you and Kate to see and tour your new schools?"

"Kind of."

"Well, we went to the high school first, for Kate. We walked into the office to meet with Kate's new counselor to figure out her schedule."

"Oh, yeah. I do remember that," I replied. "You both left me outside the office to sit on the bench and someone said, in reference to me 'Wow, they just keep getting smaller and smaller.'"

Chuckling, my dad said, "I didn't know that. Well anyways, that day they had a fight in the high school between two black students. You know how we were moving from a town that was completely white? Well, these two black students were fighting on the second floor of the high school and one of them was pushed out the window."

"Oh, yeah. I slightly remember that. Do you know why they were fighting?"

"No, but that is not the end of the story," he said. "I led with that story because of what happened next. It didn't matter at the moment that the kids who were fighting were black, but it influenced you and your fear. Your mom and I had some fear after that situation also, which led us all to make a decision."

"What are you talking about, Dad?" I asked, confused.

"Well, later in the year, when it was time for you to sign up for middle school, you asked if we would open-enroll you at another school—not the school you were supposed to go to. You were told by people at your school that it was the "bad" school. Which, looking back, probably meant it was the school that most of the black kids in town went to. We were influenced by friends and church members because we were new to the town, and so we decided to open-enroll you in a "better" school. When I thought about it, years later, I remembered that incident with the high school students. We all had that pretty fresh in our minds. The actions of those two students that day influenced our confirmation bias and, whether we were conscious of it or not, we were all influenced by it when we decided where you would go to middle school."

I had an instant lightbulb moment. "Huh—yeah, you are right! I had no idea I played into the idea of black as bad, so I did not attend the 'bad' school and decided on the school that had students who looked more like me. You are right, and it is shitty that that happened." After that comment I was silent, and the conversation ended. I was reflecting on my life as a middle school student.

After discussing race with my parents—and especially following the conversation with my dad regarding school choices—I began to think about my career as a teacher. I joined the teaching field through a program called Teach For America, which focuses on sending trained teachers to low-performing schools—which, sadly, generally means schools that are predominately attended by students of color.

Scene Jump Cut: 2007
Early childhood teaching

My first teaching job was on the southwest side of Chicago, in Little Village. I was a young, white teacher entering a preschool/day care center with four other young, white teachers placed through our program. We entered with huge amounts of control issues as extreme Type A personalities, and no understanding of the community or school culture—and we were awestruck for at least the first six months. By November, I would cry all the way to work while riding on the blue line to the pink line (the El). I was not happy and something needed to change. One of the reasons I was so unhappy was because of the interactions I was witnessing between my co-teachers and the students.

There were three adults in my classroom: I was the lead teacher, and there were two assistant teachers. One of the assistant teachers was black and the other was Latina. My two assistant teachers did not have the education required to be the lead teacher, but they had the school experience and the knowledge to help guide me in learning the culture of the community. I relied heavily on their expertise and skills in order to survive in that first year of teaching.

One of the situations I often witnessed occurred when the assistant teachers demanded the children to lie on the ground with their hands behind their back. It often went like this:

"Sy, lay on the ground. Lay down right there. Put your hands behind your back," one of my assistant teachers would say to a 4-year-old, black student. She was serious and angry because Sy had just pushed another student and then stolen a toy out of the other student's hands.

Crying, Sy lied on the ground and put his hands behind his back.

Continuing in a louder-than-normal voice, the assistant teacher said, "This—*this* is what you are going to be like if you keep this up. You are going to be laying on the ground with your hands behind your back and police looking over you. Do you want this?"

Still crying, the boy did not answer; he just lay there.

The first time I saw this happen, I was in shock. What was I witnessing? Was this something I did not understand; a part of the culture? Was this something I was going to be asked to do? I hoped not, because I was **not** going to do that. They were telling the black and brown boys in the classroom—they never did it with girls—that they were going to end up in jail; they were engraining the school-to-prison pipeline mentality into the minds of these 4-year-old children. What was happening?

While I did not stand up for Sy or any other child in the classroom that year, I did fully recognize the detrimental impact that this practice potentially had on their lives. In the moment, though, I felt like I had my own hands tied behind my back. The two assistant teachers did the same thing; I did not. I was the outsider. I did not want to come in and tell them that what they were doing was wrong. Who was I to tell them that? I was scared to stand up and did not yet know how to use my voice to advocate for my students.

When I left my first teaching job, I continued to stay in low-income and low-performing schools, which meant that I taught predominately black and brown students. In my second teaching job, I taught kindergarten for one year and second grade for one year, at a charter school in East Chicago, Indiana. I like to describe East Chicago as a suburb of Gary, Indiana, because in essence, it is in northwest Indiana and very close to the border between Illinois and Indiana. The demographics of the school building were a majority-minority, mostly black and Latino; most of the teachers were white.

During my first year at the charter school in East Chicago, I was a kindergarten teacher. One day, one of my black, male kindergarteners walked into my classroom. To be honest, he was one of my favorite students that year, even though he sometimes had days when he made good choices and he sometimes had days when he made bad choices. Interestingly, you could tell that he had already been hardened by age 5.

That particular morning when he walked in, he had picked up his breakfast in the cafeteria and was walking confidently into my classroom. As I did with all of my students, I said, "Good morning," with a bright smile. He did not smile back. That was not like him. Instead, he looked me straight in the eyes, holding a muffin in one hand and a carton of orange juice in the other, and said, "My momma told me I don't have to listen to no white lady—especially you, white lady."

Okay, so this is how my day is going to start, I thought. This was not the first time I had heard this in my few years of teaching, and I was sure it would not be my last.

Decreasing my smile a bit and cocking my head to the side, I said calmly, "Oh, wow, that is really sad to hear. But remember: In this class-room, you need to follow the rules. And in this classroom, part of that is listening to me."

"My momma said I didn't have to," he said again. "You white, and white people are not in charge of us."

"Okay," I said, realizing that I was not going to win this argument with a 5-year-old at 7:30 a.m. "Well, hopefully we can make it work today. Please go sit and eat your breakfast."

He whipped around and walked to his desk to set down his breakfast, and the day continued.

The second year at the school, I taught second grade. I was assigned to be the teacher of DeMarcus, a 10-year-old who had failed several times and in more than one grade. He was over 6 feet tall, had a temper, and knew that many of the teachers in the school building were afraid of him because he was a large, black boy who looked like a man and also had the strength of a man. He often was defiant and refused to do work in the classroom. At times he would pick up desks, as if to throw them across the room. (I never remember hearing that he actually threw a desk, though; it appeared to be more of an intimidation tactic.)

Truthfully, as a 23-year-old, 5'1", 130-pound, white teacher, I was intimidated. He scared me and he knew it. He knew I would not make him do his work. He knew that at the littlest infraction in my classroom, I would send him out. I was scared and I had no coping or redirection strategies to use with him.

One day, within the first couple weeks of school starting, he came in late and sat in his desk, which was placed at the back of the classroom by the door that led outside. He sat down in the desk—which was honestly too small for his large body—and proceeded to fall asleep, like he did every morning. However, that day I was in a different mood: I was going to "reach" this kid. I was going to make sure he did not fail again.

I walked over to his desk and said, "DeMarcus, wake up. We aren't doing this today."

He did not budge; his eyes stayed closed.

My voice got a bit louder. "DeMarcus, come on buddy, wake up." My tone was more forceful this time.

He slowly opened his eyes and turned his head to face mine, so that we were making eye contact. "Nope, stupid bitch."

Nodding my head slowly, I said, "Hmmm. Okay. Well, too bad. I am not sending you out for calling me that. Wake up and at least do this part of the lesson." I was now in the bartering stage with him.

"I know if I lift this desk up, you will send me out. Can you just send me out so I don't have to lift up the desk?"

Young and naïve, I said, "Okay, fine. Just go to the office. I will tell them you are coming."

I had given up on him. I didn't know what to do. He knew I was scared of him. He knew that most of the staff was scared of him. Was it because of his size? Was it become of his skin color? Was it a combination of the two? To this day, I am not sure. I do not know how I would have reacted if I'd had an over-6-foot white student in my classroom. Would I have behaved the same way, as a 23-year-old, novice teacher? I do know now, looking back, that I wish I would have done it differently. Knowing what I know now about African-American boys and the school system, I wish I could have reached him and not let my fear show.

That same year, due to overcrowding in the old school building, my classroom was placed in a portable classroom outside of the actual building (which is why DeMarcus sat near the door that led outside). While in this mobile classroom, the students and I often heard gunshots in the distance during lessons. One morning, I arrived at my classroom to find that its windows had been shot out the night before. Due to the gun violence they saw in their own neighborhoods, the shots we heard in the distance, and one specific morning when we arrived and the windows had bullet holes, my students and I often talked about the trauma of gun violence. I decided to create a safe space in my classroom, and about once a week, we discussed what the students needed to discuss. Often, we talked about the violence they witnessed.

One day, while scrolling through my emails during lunch, I came across an email from my administrator; in the subject line were the words, "We need to talk." I hated getting these emails. Was I in trouble? What did we need to talk about? Since it was my lunch break and I had the time, I walked down the steps of my portable building, across the parking lot, and into the school building. I walked up the stairs and down the hallway to the principal's office. When I got there, I said hello to the secretary and then knocked on the principal's door.

"Yes?" I heard her say, from inside her office.

I peeked my head around the door and said, "I got your email. I have a few minutes before I have to get my students from lunch. Do you want to talk now?"

"Oh, yeah, sure. Close the door," she said.

I closed the door and walked over to the big chair in her office, to sit down.

"So, you know that Keo isn't in school today?" Keo was one of my students. He was biracial and lived with his mom.

I nodded.

"Well, I just got some news that his mother's boyfriend—the one who was like his dad—was killed last night in a burglary." I could sense pain in her voice.

"Oh my gosh!" I was stunned. "What? Are Keo and Ky okay?" Ky was Keo's younger brother; I had worked with both of them during my two years at the charter school.

"Yes, they are both okay. They will be back tomorrow. But I just wanted to let you know, in case Keo needs to go to the counselor for any reason."

"Okay, thank you. I appreciate you telling me." With that, I walked out of her office to go pick up my students from lunch.

At the end of the school day, I began searching the internet for any information I could find. I found out that Keo's father figure, his mother's boyfriend, had entered a house to burglarize it the night before. The occupant of the house shot the intruder and killed him.

It was then that I realized that many students of color (and students living in poverty) lose out on childhood. The trauma, the experiences, and the conversations occurring in their lives create an environment that sometimes forces students to grow up faster than their counterparts who live in different parts of the country or who have a different color skin.

> *Side note: While violence can happen in any community, regardless of race, high rates of poverty lead to more violence in communities. Violence is a symptom of poverty, not a cause. When people are living in poverty, the fight-or-flight response kicks in, which results in a lack of logical thinking and causes the brain to make unethical decisions—including violence. Additionally, there are more people of color in poverty compared to white people due to historical and current discrimination, including institution and structural racism. All of that being said, while race and poverty are separated, they intertwine in communities like East Chicago, Indiana.*

A few weeks after Keo and Ky's father figure was killed in a botched robbery, I was driving home with a few colleagues after staying late to finish up some lesson plans. My colleagues and I met in Ms. T's classroom and then walked out to the parking lot together. We got in Ms. T's car, as she was the one driving us that day. She turned on her car, blasted some great '90s rap, and then began driving through the neighborhood to the interstate. (We all lived in Chicago and worked in Indiana.)

While driving, we suddenly saw police lights behind us. This was not unusual; there were often police around the neighborhood. However, we noticed that he was following us and not stopping at any of the houses, so Ms. T pulled over. The police car stopped behind our car and we saw the police officer get out. None of us knew what was going on. By the time the police officer made it to the driver's side, Ms. T had rolled down her window.

In a deep voice, the police officer said, "Ladies, what are you doing?"

Confused, Ms. T answered with a smile. "Driving home from work. We teach over at the charter school and are just heading to the interstate now."

"Oh, OK," the officer responded. "I thought it was weird for you young ladies to be traveling around here this late by yourselves. It is not safe for you to be out here when it starts to get dark. I don't mean to be harsh, but your skin color makes you stick out and that is not good past dark here, OK?"

We all nodded.

He continued, "I am going to follow you out of this neighborhood and make sure you get to the interstate." The officer's voice had changed, from a demanding tone to a softer and more caring one.

"OK, thank you, officer," we said in unison. The police officer turned around and headed back to his car while Ms. T rolled up her window. Once the window was closed, we all looked at each other with the same questioning look and just shrugged.

I finally said, "That was f****** weird." We all giggled uncomfortably and rode the rest of the ride through East Chicago in silence while the police officer followed closely behind us.

When we pulled onto the exit ramp, he honked, waved and pulled a U-turn to go back toward the charter school.

Once we were on the interstate, Ms. T said, "He does realize we work here every day, right? Like we go to those projects for home visits and we go to that store for our lunch breaks."

"Yeah. I don't know. That was weird," my other colleague said. "I am sure he meant well."

"Yeah, I am sure he did. Maybe he knows more than we do. But that *was* weird," I said.

We continued our drive home, talking about work gossip, popular television shows, and our students.

During the years I was working in East Chicago at the charter school, I met one of my best friends, Allison. She was my assigned mentor the first year, my co-cheerleading coach the second year, and a bridesmaid in my wedding several years later. She is Puerto Rican and has darker skin than I do. Honestly, she and Ahmad have the same beautiful, caramel-colored skin.

When I met her, I was a single mom. I often would sleep at her house on the weekends after partying or hang out with her during the day, bringing Ahmad along, too. At this point in her life she did not have any of her own kids, but was a teacher, so she enjoyed having Ahmad around at different events for school or just for an afternoon lunch at a local restaurant. Often, while we were in public together with Ahmad, we had a recurring experience.

After ordering our food at Panera, Allison, Ahmad, and I made our way to a table. Allison got up to fill her drink cup while I waited at the table with Ahmad. When Allison came back, I took my cup to the soda machine. Waiting for our buzzer to buzz, indicating that our food was ready, a woman walked up to us and looked directly at Allison.

"He is beautiful boy. How old is he?" she asked, smiling. She was looking only at Allison and not even indicating that she saw me at the table.

Shrugging, Allison looked at me and said, "I don't know, how old is he?"

Now also smiling, and realizing what was happening, I politely responded, "He is a little over 1 year old."

Somewhat startled that I answered, the woman's eyebrows raised and she said, "Oh, well, he is cute." She walked away without any other conversation.

Once she was gone, Allison said, "People think I am his mom all the time. I know it's because we have the same color skin, but it always throws me off when I get asked about him when I am with you."

"Yeah, I know. People are ignorant sometimes," I said. "They either think we are a couple or have no idea how to get their foot out of their mouth because they assumed he was yours based purely on his skin color."

Yet, knowing that this was not the first or the last time situations like this would happen in my life, what could I do? Educate every person I ever encounter? At this point in my life, as a newly divorced, single mother, I was tired. I would find my energy and I would find my voice, but as a 20-something, I was tired and knew that I had a long life of racial questioning ahead of me.

Scene Jump Cut: 2011
Peoria, Illinois

After four years of living in Chicago, I knew that it was time to move. I wanted to be closer to my parents. I had recently gotten divorced and was looking forward to having my parents around, to help raise Ahmad.

When I moved, I got a teaching job in one of the towns that had sundown laws in its recent history. Additionally, the school I got a job at was experiencing a demographic change, with more students of color entering at an increasing rate. The conversations I heard the veteran white teachers have in the teachers' lounge were often racist and judgmental. A summary of a comment I often heard was, "The kids are just getting so bad. We have never had students like this before. They don't listen, they talk back, and their parents just don't care. Ten years ago our students were different and not as bad." What I don't know if they realized is that 10 years ago, there were no students of color in their classrooms. The difference? Students of color were entering the school building and, from my perspective, implicit biases were clouding the views of many of the teachers.

My second year at the school, when I was feeling more confident in myself as an educator, there was a black boy who often made choices in his first-grade classroom that resulted in his teacher kicking him out. Seeing him in the office daily, I began to talk to him. My principal noticed that the boy was calm when he was with me, so he began to send him to my classroom instead of making him sit in the office.

Through daily visits to my classroom, I realized that no one was getting to know this boy; no one was trying to understand the cause behind his behavior, and no one seemed to care that he had different life experiences and made choices differently than the other students in the classroom. My aide and I got to know him, though. We learned, through conversations, that he missed his dad, who left and often did not show up for visitation. We learned that his mother was often gone because she had to work. We learned that he did not feel like he had any friends because the teacher always sent him out. We learned a lot about him. And, whenever he was in our room, he finished all of his work and then began helping us with our pre-kindergarten students. He was making progress.

While I would like to report that he made great strides and that we changed his life, that is not what happened. Eventually, the principal stopped sending him to my classroom and he was sent to the alternative school because of his behavior—behavior that would not have happened if teachers just took the time to get to know him and did not judge him based on his skin color and life experiences. While I cannot guarantee that he was sent to the alternative school just because of implicit biases based on his skin color, I cannot shake the feeling that that is one of the main reasons he was labeled as a "bad kid."

While I was teaching pre-kindergarten in my new city, I began dating Doug. We met on Match.com. We messaged each other several times before meeting for dinner and drinks. Reflecting on our online courtship, Doug always found one email I sent quite odd. In my view, though, I needed to send him this communication before meeting because of multiple negative experiences I'd had with people in the past.

> *Evening,*
>
> *Yeah, I have one sister who is married with three little ones (7, 4, 7 months), and they live in the Quad Cities, so we see them pretty often. My family is very small but close-knit. Well, the immediate family is. My son is actually biracial and when he was born/I was married, we lost contact with some family members because of racial tensions, but my parents and my sister's family and I are all very close. I am actually staying at my parents' house tonight because my dad is at the Cubs' game with my nephew and my son wanted to have a sleepover with Mimi (my mom!) :) My son is actually with me 100 percent of the time. His dad lives in Chicago and could see him but chooses not to, so I don't argue with that. My dad has really taken on the father-figure role for him, but it's still hard, though. You and your ex-wife seem to have had a very amicable divorce. When my son and I go to St. Louis I am planning on the zoo one day, and then there is a Children's Museum or something for the second day. It is hard though because you have to figure in nap time ... and we do not want to skip nap time (for mommy either! :))*
>
> *Have a good one.*
>
> *Anni*

Other than the fact that I am a smiley person, and want that to come across in written communication, he found it odd that I mentioned that my son was biracial.

When we were talking about this during the writing of this book, Doug reflected, "At the time, I just figured you had had some experiences where people were not okay with it, so I thought it was weird, but didn't put too much thought into it. I mean, I did not feel it necessary to tell you my two daughters are twins and white."

Doug grew up in a small town in Central Illinois. When discussing race and his experience with diversity on one of our first dates, he said, "I did not see my first person of color until I was in middle school, and that was just through sports. There was not diversity where I grew up." The town where he grew up could be described as a "white-house, picket-fence" community. While there is diversity today, the rooted mentality of racism is still present among many citizens.

Aside from the community he grew up in, Doug's family also influenced his views and experiences. Doug identifies himself as "liberal, but learning." As is evident through many of this book's stories, however, he often picks up on underlying and judgmental meanings to conversations we have in the community before I do. Still, one of the biggest areas of contention between us is standing up to his family—especially for Ahmad.

When Ahmad is not included or is ignored at certain family functions, we cannot tell if it stems from a step-family/blended family issue, or if it implicit racism. Either way, standing up for Ahmad is one of our main goals. We have decided that if something racist is said within earshot of Ahmad, we will say something and/or leave the family event. However, there are other things that happen that do not directly impact him, so we choose not to say anything. In the near future, though, I can see more honest conversations occurring.

Do I know how to breach the subject and have more honest conversations about race? Nope. Additionally, my personal racial anxiety and the fear of reactions leaves me paralyzed. Therefore, crossing the divide—between others being "stuck in their ways" or "not meaning anything by it," to truly understanding the impact of their actions—is hard to do.

What does this mean for Ahmad's future in interacting with his family and friends? I don't know. But we make sure to have constant conversations with Ahmad and to keep a "you can ask me anything" policy, because we know there will be a time when he questions or feels uncomfortable—and while we may not have the answer immediately, we will sure as hell get him what he needs and have open conversations about it. We will support him in his journey of racial identity in our family and in the wider society.

Doug is Ahmad's dad in every sense of the word besides genes, and he has shown his dedication to raising a son—a black son—in a world that treats and views black men differently. He understands the need for role models, for exposure, and for acceptance—not just tolerance. Doug instills this through both actions and words.

For example, when we get in the car, Ahmad will routinely ask everyone what superhero or wrestler they want to be.

"Dad, what superhero do you want to be?" Ahmad excitedly said from the backseat one day, while on the way to a birthday party.

"Umm, I will be Black Panther. He was awesome in that movie," Doug said. "Who do you want to be?"

"I want to be …" Ahmad took a long pause as he thought. "Wolverine!"

"Awesome."

"Dad, what wrestler do you want to be?" Ahmad asked, excitedly.

"I want to be John Cena because your mom thinks he's hot," Doug answered. He smiled and gave a small laugh.

"Yeah, she does. That is so weird. I want to be Triple H. Who do you think would win?"

While interviewing Doug for this book, I asked him about things that stuck out to him regarding Ahmad, specifically. One of the things he reflected on was the superhero-and-wrestler conversations.

"I am always very conscientious of choosing both black and white superheroes and wrestlers when we play that game," Doug said, matter-of-factly. "Ahmad doesn't seem to pick based on skin color and I make sure I do not, either."

As my eyebrows raised and my head nodded, I said, "Oh, that makes sense."

He continued, "Oh—that reminds me of something Evie said the other day." (Evie and Olivia are Doug's twin daughters from his first marriage. They live with us half of the time. They are legally Ahmad's sisters since the adoption.)

"What?" I asked.

"She was telling me about a new little girl in her school and she was describing the new little girl's hair and clothes. She told me her name and then she said something that I think you would love and also find interest-ing," Doug said. "She said, 'She doesn't have skin like Livie or me, she has beautiful skin like Ahmad.'"

A huge smile spread across my face. "Really, she said that? That is so sweet."

"Yeah, I thought so, also."

Race is an interesting concept. It comes into all of our lives but is actu-ally not based in anything scientific. Race is also interesting because there is so much hate in our country based on race.

Where does hate come from? Where does hate come from, specifically, based on racial differences? If you do a Google search for "how to talk to children about race," you will get over 288,000,000 hits. That is evidence that there is not a one-size-fits-all understanding of how to effectively talk to children about race in order to reduce the hate in our country.

Everyone has different opinions, experiences, life lessons, and facts. However, as a mother, I base my expertise on a Nelson Mandela quote: "People must learn to hate, and if they can learn to hate, they can be taught to love, for love comes more naturally to the human heart than its opposite ... Man's goodness is a flame that can be hidden but never extin-guished." We can all be taught to love.

Reflecting on this quote, and President Obama's book, *Dreams From My Father*, I wrote this blog post about hate in 2014:

> *How do we learn to hate? Some people base their views on facts from child development; others blame it on a low self-esteem; some people blame it on parents and the ones who raise child; still others blame it on fear. Everyone seems to have his or her own opinion, and so do I. I believe we learn to hate from experiences, from fear, from our parents, from our society, and, most recently, from the media that is constantly blasting news to children, parents, grandparents, and teachers about the hate in America and around the world.*
>
> *Teachers, however, are the individuals that stick out to me the most— maybe because I am one, or maybe because of my current research focus. Either way, teachers are seen in our society as needing to have "values" and "education" beyond the lives of the children they are teaching.*

As a classroom teacher, I have seen children hate. I have heard children hate. I have felt children hate through the sadness in another one's eyes. We do learn to hate, but from where? Everywhere.

I recently finished research focusing on multicultural education in classrooms and how school administration and teachers address the "tough," "taboo" topics of multicultural education: sexuality, race, religion, gender, ability, age, etc. And what I found is uneasiness among teachers. A fear. A "if I don't talk about it, then it won't be true." Or "that's not my reality, so we can just skip over that." Which, through gleaning other research, is true in many areas of the country and across grade levels in education. We cannot ignore the fact that the demographics in the United States are changing. Twenty years ago, looking at the elementary students singing in front of our Presbyterian church, you would see only middle- to upper-class, white children. That is not the case anymore. You look up to our chancel area today and you will see maybe one white child up there, singing their heart out, while the other children are "children of color," who were also signing their hearts out.

We must talk. We must listen. We must ask questions. Our society is changing and if we refuse to change with it, our children will be left to fend for themselves in a world where hate is screamed at them daily.

Regardless of your experiences, my experiences, or America's experiences, it is important to remember that race and racism were invented by people who wanted to categorize, judge, and gain power and control over others. Therefore, the definition of racism actually differs by group and is often a point of dispute. However, I also remember that race is not a biological category, but rather a social and cultural category. Therefore, the hate we see based on race is purely learned. Hate is learned, and therefore, love can be learned. To have a next generation of love, it is my job—our job—to advocate and speak out against hate and to practice love and acceptance.

10

Education

"The schools were not pressed to begin the desegregation process by the courts, the federal government, or the State of Illinois; rather, the districts' efforts to desegregate were locally initiated and generally approved by Peoria's citizens, civil rights leadership, the business community, the school board, and the educators."

U.S. Commission on Civil Rights, 1977

"The schools in America today (2018) are more segregated than when Martin Luther King Jr. was murdered. Our public-school system sees black and brown children as violent, disruptive, unpredictable, and future criminals."

Ijemo Oluo, 2018

Scene Jump Cut: 2012

"No, you don't understand. I have to get him into a good school. The research shows that if he does not get into a good school now, his whole life could be different."

By this point in the conversation, I was exasperated and on the verge of frantic.

My father was sitting on the couch in my living room, having put Ahmad to bed for the night. He was there to watch Ahmad so I could attend night classes for my doctorate degree. That night in class we had talked about the opportunity gap, not the achievement gap, in schools for black students. Black students are disproportionally given fewer opportunities, which is usually mistaken for the "achievement gap" between minority and majority groups.

Straightforward, and a little exhausted himself, my dad said, "Anni. He will be fine. He has a very smart mother. He is excelling now. He will be fine wherever you choose to send him for preschool. This is not the end of the world."

By this time, it was close to 9:30 at night. I had just driven over an hour to get home and my dad was at the end of a long day. We were both too tired to keep the conversation going. My dad stood up from the couch, kissed me on the forehead and said, "You will make the right decision. Ahmad is lucky to have you as a mom." He opened the front door and walked down the steps to his car. I closed the door behind him, locked it, and turned off the outside light. It was time for me to go to bed. Worrying about where I was going to start Ahmad's education—which preschool to choose for him—could wait until the next day.

As an educator dedicated to children and their future, I have always concentrated my research, passion, and advocacy on closing the opportunity gap. After returning from Kenya and having worked with street boys, I knew that there were children in America who also were experiencing poverty, loneliness, absent parents, and disproportionately lacking opportunities—just as I had seen in Kenya. So I went into education, with the goal of changing the world one starfish* at a time. (*The Starfish Story is at the beginning of the book.)

Since 2006, my time in the field of education has allowed me to be a lifelong learner, which has influenced my personal growth. Through research focused on oppressed populations in school districts—from zero-tolerance policies, to student resource officers (SRO), to curricular changes to racial biases embedded in the institution of schools—I have gained knowledge. Yet I desire to keep learning from others. My future progress in this is, without a doubt, rooted in both my childhood experiences and in my life as a parent.

Scene Jump Cut: 2017

Driving to work one day, I was listening to a podcast hosted by DeRay Mckesson, called *Pod Save the People*. I heard DeRay state that in his family, he is a third-generation reader. Though I was driving more than 70 miles per hour down the highway, I grabbed a pen and piece of paper to jot down that statement, so I could come back to it later. I wrote "third-generation reader" in sloppy handwriting.

When I arrived at work, I parked my car but kept the ignition running. I looked down at the piece of paper where I had sloppily written, "third-generation reader." I began to reflect: What type of structural racism is embedded into schools that resulted in a man in his 30s being a third-generation reader? I sat in my car for a little while longer as I jotted down more notes, mostly reflecting on my own family's history. I realized, not for the first time, that I have privileges—my family has privileges—because of our history. Our country has a history of providing educational opportunities to white people, whether through providing funding for school through the GI Bill or providing the opportunity to own land—something that financially supported my sister and me through college, so that we could attend and graduate with little to no student debt.

Scene Jump Cut
Family history

The educational history of my family might mirror that of many white Americans whose families immigrated to America many generations ago and were able to purchase large amounts of land. Interestingly, my paternal and maternal families had quite different experiences, which were based primarily on their economic situation. My maternal side had experiences rich in education, money, and land ownership; my paternal side, though not as financially fortunate, was rooted in a desire to learn—even when economic hardships were overwhelming.

I gained knowledge about the two sides of my family through stories and interviews. While all of my grandparents have passed away, my parents have stories of our family history that begin in 1938—many generations after our family put down roots in America.

In 1938, compulsory education and child labor laws were signed. By this point in my maternal great-grandparents' lives, they had experienced formal education. My great-grandmother, Ida Potter, attended school in a one-room schoolhouse until she was 13 years old. On her 13th birthday, she began working 13- to 14-hour days at the phone company. My maternal great-grandfather traveled more than 60 miles daily to attend the Normal Teaching School, one of the first teacher preparation programs in Illinois. He received his teaching degree after six months of schooling and later married my great-grandmother, who was one of his former students in his one-room schoolhouse. My maternal grandmother received her master's degree in education and was the principal of an elementary school for many years. My maternal grandfather received his bachelor's

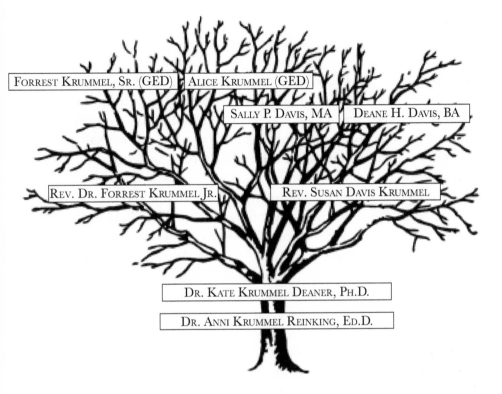

FORREST KRUMMEL, SR. (GED)   ALICE KRUMMEL (GED)

SALLY P. DAVIS, MA   DEANE H. DAVIS, BA

REV. DR. FORREST KRUMMEL JR.   REV. SUSAN DAVIS KRUMMEL

DR. KATE KRUMMEL DEANER, PH.D.

DR. ANNI KRUMMEL REINKING, ED.D.

degree and ran his own business, which was not the first family business owned by my maternal family.

While my maternal family excelled in school, owned land, and had experiences that built a firm economic foundation for our family, my paternal great-grandparents had different experiences. Due to economic hardships, they were not provided the same educational opportunities. Instead of attending school regularly, they worked as tenant farmers, receiving education in the form of "street smarts" or knowledge of how to run a farm. When the child labor laws were signed, they were too old to formally attend school; however, they understood the importance of school. They made sure that their children had the benefits that they were denied: the ability to attend formal school. That goal was never reached, though, due to economic hardships and parental deaths.

Both of my paternal grandparents lost their parents at an early age, lived in rural Illinois, and had siblings to care for. When the Depression hit America in the early 1940s, my grandparents had no other choice but to drop out of school and go to work because they were in charge of caring for and supporting their younger siblings. When my grandfather turned 17, he enlisted in the Navy by lying about his age. He was in the Navy for several years. Upon his return to Illinois, he met and married my grandmother. Since they both had been denied the opportunity to attend high school, they worked hard to receive their GEDs after the birth of my father, their only child. They were fulfilling the goal set by their parents and grandparents a generation earlier—attending and completing a formal education.

Growing up as the daughter of two formally educated college graduates, my mother was destined to continue that tradition. Before attending college, however, she vividly remembers her experiences in high school—specifically when her high school desegregated. Although *Oliver Brown et al. v. Board of Education of Topeka, Shawnee County, Kansas, et al.* (more commonly known as *Brown v. Board of Education*) was decided in the mid-1950s, parts of the country were slow to desegregate. In the late 1960s and early 1970s, my mother's high school finally became desegregated. She was a student at the time and remembers police officer coming to their school daily to help break up fights. She remembers being scared to walk down certain hallways because that was where "all the black students hung out." She remembers being harassed by black girls as she was walking to class, but choosing to ignore the comments and not engage in any sort of conversation. She remembers the desegregation—and that experience has most likely influenced several of her life choices.

My father, growing up as the only son of two blue-collar workers, had more opportunities then other children in his neighborhood. His parents consciously made the decision to have only one son so that they could both provide economic stability in his life and have the finances available to work toward their own formal education. This determination and economic stability paid off for their son, and when my dad was in his early 30s, he received his terminal degree, or the highest degree awarded in a given field—a degree his parents lived to witness. He had earned a doctorate in theology.

My father was not the only one to earn a degree beyond his bachelor's; my mother received her master's degree in theology and supported my father while he worked on his doctorate. The deep-rooted dedication to educational achievement and the support in our family arguably hit a peak when both of my parents' daughters achieved terminal degrees in education, with minimal to no student loans. Their daughters—my sister and I—were provided the privilege of not only educational achievement, but also economic stability—sometimes referred to as generational wealth. While the institutions set up in America and the opportunities to build strong foundations of wealth helped our family, we also have a strong determination to embrace education and instill the value of lifelong learning in our children.

While this is my background and explanation of privilege, how does it influence my life as a white mother navigating a racist society and educational system? Due to privileges and the family Ahmad was born into, he will not be a third-generation reader; he will be a fifth-generation, college-educated, black man. This is purely coincidental and not based on anything he has done so far in his life. He has built-in privileges because of who he is. However, America sees him differently. School systems and the institutional racism built into schools see him differently.

While it is hard to accept, American schools are built on racist foundations that are often hard to decipher when procedures and practices are "what we have always done."

I suggest we change our perception of statistics. Focus on the fact that almost 2 percent of Americans have a doctoral degree, and 1.5 percent have earned a professional degree that requires study beyond a four-year bachelor's course. Furthermore, doctorates earned by blacks or African Americans has risen from 6.2 percent in 2005 to 6.5 percent in 2015. Education is not only based in doctorate degrees, either, as many Americans know—the high school completion and graduation rate among African Americans has been on the rise for years. Although this is a great accomplishment for our country, statistically, it is important to also realize how recently school segregation was still rampant—and, arguably, still is today.

At the time of writing this book, Ahmad is in third grade. While I am very aware that we still have years of schooling ahead of us, the experiences, fears, and reflections I have had to this point have influenced the way I interact with his school. What I have come to realize is that "book-smart" and "street-smart" are two completely separate things. While I always knew this unconsciously, it did not become apparent until Ahmad began having encounters outside of family life.

Before Ahmad began kindergarten, my husband and I made the conscious decision to move houses—for space, but also to stay in the district of the city I had lived in for a few years, by that point. It was the city where my parents grew up and now lived. We were aware of the "white flight" that had been occurring for several years and did not want to be part of that wave. We consciously chose to stay in the district that gets the response of, "Oh, you go *there*?" Or, "Oh, I would never send my kids to that district." While these might be the responses from many white parents, the district has one of the best high schools in Illinois. The view of the district being "bad" was predominately based on statistics.

In this district, 21.7 percent of the student body self-identifies as white and 57.1 percent self-identifies as black. Additionally, the district houses one of the lowest median household income levels in the entire state of Illinois—and in the country. It is known as the second-worst place for African Americans to live, as reported by the *Wall Street Journal* in 2017. However, all of those statistics are just that—statistics. My son is in a classroom that, demographically, looks like a classroom of the future. He is in the majority, as a socially perceived black boy (by 2044, it's estimated that schools will be majority-minority). He is developing academic and social skills that will benefit him in the reality of the real world—a diverse world.

In the first semester of kindergarten, before anyone really knew each other, Ahmad came home from school with a question. I had picked him up at the walk-up door and we were waiting for the crossing guard to stop passing cars. Ahmad looked up and me and said, "Mom, what does 'you better back up off' mean?" By this point, we had crossed the street and were walking home, hand-in-hand. We only lived about a block from the school, so on nice days we enjoyed walking together and catching up. It was typical for him to have a question or a comment on our walk home, but this question took me a second to respond.

Pausing for just a moment, I said, "What? What do you mean? Where did you hear that?"

"Well, today Damari told me in line to 'back up off.' What does that mean?" he asked.

Smiling at him, I said, "Oh, sweetie. That just means he wanted you to back up a little bit. Maybe you were in his space?"

He shrugged. "Oh, okay. Well then, why didn't he just say, 'Could you back up a little?' I didn't know what to do when he said that, so I just stared at him and then the other boys started to make fun of me."

Staying calm, I said, "Oh, okay. Well, next time, it just means to back up a little bit." The conversation ended and we walked the rest of the way home, hand-in-hand and silent.

A few years later, I was listening to the podcast *Code Switch*. An 11-year-old girl reflected on her development of language as a black girl being raised by a white mother, through adoption. "EDILOWEE: So a while back, my mom taught me about how to identify whether or not a white person was calling me the N-word in a racist way, or a black person was saying it in a friendly way, in a welcoming way. And I came back from school, and it was a school of all black people. And I said, Mama, a black boy called me the N-word. And I was so excited about it. And I told her I did the checklist. I looked for all the signs. He said my in the beginning. There was ah instead of an er. And he was black. And he smiled while he said it. And I was so happy because I felt like I had finally belonged in a black space." While hearing this 11-year-old girl talk about her experience, I could see this same experience play out in my household one day.

While Ahmad's question about "back up off" was not the only time he brought home a question from school, hearing that podcast I knew our experience was not unique. During his first few weeks of kindergarten, he often had questions about what boys were talking about because he did not understand the slang they were using. Over the years, as he would ask about more comments, I would come to realize that he was learning some key things in life that many people will, in the future, perceive that he knows and has experienced. While these assumptions may not be apparent or even true, they are the concepts that run through my head when a question like the one above comes up. I have gained these perspectives through my own life experiences, many of which have been described in this book:

1. Always greet everyone when you walk into a room, especially in a gathering of friends and/or family.

2. Some jargon or words are going to be used with or around you, and that is okay, but they cannot be used by your father or me.

3. Some handshakes or greetings are going to be used in reference to you, but not to your father or me.

4. People are going to see you differently—police may be mean, store clerks may follow you, and doctors may not believe your pain, but you have done nothing wrong. It is their prejudices, not your actions.

In my perspective, this is a type of "code-switching," or what I have heard referred to as "being a cultural chameleon." Essentially, code-switching—for the definition I am referring to—means that a person is able to alternate between two or more languages or language varieties, as well as switch between cultural codes or unspoken rules. Becoming a cultural chameleon does not happen overnight. It takes experience, exposure, sometimes uncomfortable conversations, and the willingness to be open. However, I have witnessed my own son diving between a culture and language he knows and a cultural and language variety he is uncomfortable with. Am I failing, as a mother of a biracial son?

That conversation on the walk home, during one of Ahmad's first weeks of school, has stuck with me. There have been other, similar situations, as Ahmad made it through each year in school, but by now the teachers in the school know him; the kids in his class know him; and the parents know him. He is not judged based on his skin color, but rather on his character and his serious and shy personality—and that makes me happy.

Although there have been negative experiences in his school life, the positive experiences outweigh the negative. His school—the school in the district that people are scared of—is one of the more progressive schools I have interacted with. (Keep in mind that I interact with a lot of schools as a professor of early childhood education.) Ahmad's school teaches the *real* history of America, and encourages questions. Students learn the *real* history of people hating Martin Luther King Jr., when he was alive; and of pilgrims stealing from the Native Americans. They learn the real history that should be taught everywhere in America, so that it may influence our future in such a way that everyone truly understands the oppression that has occurred for centuries.

Personal Blog Post: February 2017

"Hey, Mom. Do you know who made the flag?"

"Yes. Betsy Ross. Why?"

"Oh, man. I knew that. We learned about it today in school."

"Where did you learn that? Who taught you that?"

"We have these books that tell us about lots of different people." (The Who Was book series.)

This is how the conversation with my 7-year-old son started, the other day after school. As an educator and researcher who focuses on multicultural curriculum implementation, I was excited to continue this conversation with my son.

Twenty years ago, when I was in elementary school—or even four years ago, when I was still teaching in a classroom setting—I was paralyzed by my own fear of teaching the "real" history of our nation. Would I make parents mad? Would I have the support of the administration? I longed to teach the history that has, for so long, been silenced in our nation; the hidden curriculum in schools that, for so many years, was one of silence, heteronormativity, and ignorance. While many schools still embody this mentality today, I wanted to continue to learn what my son's public school was teaching—a public school that represents many ethnicities, races, cultures, religions, sexualities, and overall identities.

My son continued to tell me the story of Harriet Tubman helping slaves escape. He learned that a white man threw something to stop the slaves and it hit her in the head, making her sick for many days. My son learned about (and is doing research on) Frederick Douglass. He described him as a man who looked like him, with brown skin, and was a slave who escaped. My son was also very interested in the fact that Douglass did not know when he was actually born, but that he had to estimate his birthday. (We discussed why this was.) My son continued to talk about Rosa Parks getting in trouble for not giving a white man her seat, and about Martin Luther King Jr. He told me that MLK was killed by someone who was mad because he was changing the laws for black people. He was saying that black people are people, too. When I asked him who was teaching him all of this, he flatly said, "Everyone. In music, we sing a song about Peg Leg Joe who told the slaves how and where to escape. He had a boat and he helped the slaves escape. He also told the slaves to follow the Big Dipper to continue to travel north. In technology, I am doing research on Frederick Douglass. In our classroom, we have lots of books about people."

While we were having this conversation, I remembered something that had happened around Christmastime one year. We were driving to church, and there was a cross lit up on the top of someone's house. We talked about why people put crosses up at Christmastime (from our Christian lens). Then my son said, "Jewish people don't celebrate Christmas." We do not have any close Jewish friends or family members, so again, I was shocked. I said, very calmly, "You are right. How do you know that?" Ahmad replied quickly. "Oh, we learned about it in music class the other day. They get lots of presents, but not for Christmas."

This. This is what teaching looks like. This is what teaching sounds like. This is what teaching feels like. It feels inclusive. It is honesty about our nation's history. It is student projects focused on Frederick Douglass, Martin Luther King Jr., and the unsung black, female heroes of NASA.

While the facts may not be solidifying in a 7-year-old's mind, at least they are the truth. I can only hope that as he continues to attend school in this district, the teachers will remain empowered and supported. I pray that his teachers continue to teach the true history of the United States and not some watered-down version—the version I learned growing up, that included Martin Luther King Jr., as a person whom everyone loved; a version of history that never spoke about anything outside of the heteronormative view. The way in which my son's school—and, I would hope, other schools in the district—is teaching multicultural topics, my son is not fearful of race discussions. My son is not apprehensive about the statement facts concerning beatings that happened in our history, or the differences among and between religions. They are facts, they are real life, and they are part of his world.

In 2018, Ahmad was a third grader. As he and I were walking home from school, he turned to me and said, "We talked about the kneeling today."

Holding hands, just like we did in kindergarten, I turned to him and said, "You mean the NFL and Colin Kaepernick stuff?"

"Yeah. We talked about it today during enrichment. The teacher asked us to write if we think the NFL players should be able to kneel during the national anthem."

"Oh, did the teacher tell you why they are kneeling?"

He looked up at me and said, "Umm, I think it has to do something with Trump. He is not a nice man."

Supporting that response, but furthering his knowledge, I said, "Well, kind of. Actually, it started because of police brutality. Police officers are killing black men and women at a higher rate than white people."

"Oh."

"What did you write about?" I asked him. "Do you think the players should be able to kneel?" I was curious to see what he wrote. I know he had heard his dad and me talking about it at home, so I wondered what he picked up.

"Oh, yeah. I wrote that they should be able to. They are not doing anything wrong," he said, matter-of-factly.

"Cool. What did your teacher say?"

"Nothing really. Some of the other students thought the same as me. I think only one student didn't think that way. The teacher never told us what she thought."

"Okay. Well, I did that same activity with my college students last night," I said. That semester I was teaching a diverse learners course, and I tried to bring in current events as a way to help my students understand how to have difficult conversations with their own students one day.

"That's cool. What did they think?"

"Well, I had some students think the players shouldn't be able to kneel and I had some—even military veterans—say that it was okay. Many people wrote that we are free in America and that kneeling is a freedom of speech."

Nodding in response to my statement, Ahmad typed in our code to raise the garage door and we both walked inside to get a snack.

Outside of my experience as a parent, I also have devoted my life's professional and personal goals to understanding and eradicating educational inequity. My research focuses on multicultural topics, including race. Therefore, many of my lectures and courses as a professor focus on my personal and professional experiences on the topic of race. During one of my lectures with a new group of students, I began talking about implicit and explicit biases. I talked about my son and my experiences as a mother to a socially perceived black son.

After the class, one student came up to me. All of the other students had left by this point. She was a non-traditional student in her mid-30s, African-American, a mother and a wife.

Standing at the table, her on one side and me on the other, she looked me in the eyes and said, "Let me tell you something, Dr. Reinking. When you started to talk today all I thought was 'Oh, Lord. Here is another white lady with a black son about to preach some bull to us.'"

I smiled awkwardly, not knowing where this was going.

She continued, "But you know what you're talking about. You know your shit, and I have some questions."

I breathed a sigh of relief. I have had other black women walk up to me and start a conversation in a similar fashion, but it did not end that well. My student began to ask me about schools in the St. Louis area and how my husband and I had made the decision of where to send my son to school. After I answered all of her questions, I told her to have a great evening. We both went our respective ways.

That night in class, I had begun to introduce some of the key research I wanted to make sure my teacher candidates understood:

1. The school-to-prison pipeline is part of the institutional racism embedded in school mindsets and procedures. Over the years, white suspensions have stayed the same while black student suspensions have tripled. Black students are not "worse than"

white students, but at times, black students are perceived through a different reality.

2. There is no such thing as a 30-million word gap. The study this statistic is based on is controversial and was not completed in a way that facilitates the development of a generalizable conclusion. The study included 42 families over 40 years ago and has failed replication. The study has been cited over 8,000 times and therefore has become a common reference in the field of education when discussing children of color and/or children living in poverty.

Side note: The 30-million-word gap continues the tradition of blaming low-income communities of color for their own marginalization. It suggests that parents and caregivers who are confronting the many barriers produced by generations of racialized poverty, including lack of decent jobs, affordable housing, health care, and food security can undo their racialized poverty if they just used more words with their children. It amounts to looking victims of generations of racial oppression straight in the eyes and saying "let them eat words." It also absolves the broader society from addressing the structural racism that lies at the root of the marginalization of low-income communities of color. @ theducationallingustic, 2018

3. The claim that prisons are planned according to black male third-grade reading scores has been found to be mostly a myth. However, there is a strong connection between low early literacy skills and our country's exploding incarceration rates, primarily among African-American men.

4. Discipline policies, including zero-tolerance policies and school resource officers (SROs), are actually doing the opposite of their intended purpose. Zero-tolerance policies create an environment where students are suspended or expelled at higher rates, rather than helping the students get back on track. Furthermore, black students were almost four times more likely than white students to be suspended. Additionally, SROs have actually created an environment in which students of color—specifically girls of

color—are four times more likely than white girls to get arrested at school. These discipline policies are creating schools that treat students as if they are already in a prison and need to be controlled. They are also damaging students' self-confidence and self-esteem. The current movement in schools focuses on restorative practice as a way to help build positive relationships and logically hold students accountable for their actions.

Overall, through Ahmad's experiences in school and my own research, I truly believe in the challenge set forth in the field of education: school boards, administrators, teachers, and policymakers need to challenge the legitimacy of white-centered, Eurocentric educational curriculum and policies, because the reality of American history is our country's true foundation.

Finally, as a mother who understands (and is sometimes guilt-ridden by) privilege, I am a strong advocate for racial bias training in school buildings. If Starbucks can shut down all of their stores nationwide and hire an African-American female as their COO, after backlash from racism that was experienced and documented in a few of their stores, then school districts can do the same. Employees at Starbucks are not the only individuals in the country with implicit biases; everyone has implicit biases. Therefore, providing *quality* training to teachers is essential to breaking the cycle of school-experienced racism.

Teachers are at the foundation of our children's lives. They are role models, and when role models either display racist behaviors or combat racist behavior, entire school communities can change. The manner in which teachers act and speak influences both how students of color feel in a school community and the actions and words of other students in a school community. Becoming aware of our own biases, through training and self-reflection, can change the trajectory of schools—and our children's lives.

11

Role Models

*"**Black Panther** is important because little black boys and girls will watch it and have a role model that looks just like them to aspire to. They will know that their skin color is valuable and that they can achieve greatness as well."*

Wilkinson, 2016

"Black people have historically been, and continue to be, underrepresented, misrepresented, or invisible in children's literature. Black male characters are even less visible, and even fewer still, are books reflecting positive and empowered depictions of black boys."

Moms of Black Boys United

Scene Jump Cut: Circa 2018

Sipping a cup of coffee at McDonald's, Frosty asked, "How are you guys doing this week?" He was sitting with two gentlemen he met with regularly, usually once a month. They were all local ministers and found their monthly meetings helpful and supportive.

After wiping off their faces and swallowing their chosen breakfast meal, they both responded with a nicety: "Good."

"Well, that's good," Frosty responded, taking another sip of his black coffee; no cream, no sugar.

These three gentlemen had been meeting together for years as collegiate pastors who talk about everyday life, pastoral life, and anything else that comes up. Frosty—my dad—is a Presbyterian pastor and is white. Paul is a Baptist pastor and is black. Elijah is a Free Methodist pastor and is black. They consciously began meeting with the intention to educate, close the divide, and, most importantly, just become friends.

They continued to talk on that beautiful Tuesday morning, drinking cups of coffee, eating breakfast, and discussing current events. In the town they all lived in, there had recently been several shootings. One case involved an unarmed black man being shot by a white police officer. This event did not make national news, though, and the citizens of the community did not take to the streets and protest like people had after the similar shooting in Ferguson, Missouri. (*Note: Since the time of the shooting, the American Civil Liberties Union has filed a lawsuit against the city and the police officer.*)

Elijah turned to the two gentlemen he was sitting with and said, "The man was shot, but there were no protests. I think a lot of it has to do with all the work we do to close the divide, the racial divide, in this town."

Frosty and Paul both nodded in agreement and took sips of coffee.

"It's hard being a black man in America," Paul said.

"I need to learn. I need role models to help me educate my grandson," Frosty added. This was not a new train of conversation for these three gentlemen. They often talked about race and they often spoke of Ahmad.

"Well, you can't let him go to the playground," Paul said bluntly.

"What? What do you mean, we 'can't let him go to the playground'?"

Elijah put down his breakfast and spoke up. "Yeah, playgrounds are bad places, especially as he gets older. He can get in with the wrong people there. Nothing good happens at a playground for young black boys." He was looking Frosty directly in the eyes at this point.

"Yeah, and things like Tamir Rice can happen. People get scared of black boys, even when they are just playing—playing the same way little white boys do," Paul chimed in.

Taking a moment to "reflect and ponder," as Frosty likes to say, the silence was finally broken when Frosty said, "Oh, I guess I never thought of it like that."

The other two men went back to eating and drinking. Frosty took a few more minutes to write down his thoughts so that he could come back to them at a later point, and then also went back to sipping his coffee.

The conversation did not end there. The three ministers continued to talk, catch up on life, and share news of people and things to pray for. At one point in the conversation, Frosty interjected.

"You know Ahmad's barber? Well, his son is in prison. I have been writing to him. I would like to pray about him. He just got out of solitary confinement," Frosty said.

After a few more prayer requests were voiced, the conversation turned back to Ahmad's barber.

Paul told Frosty, "It's good you take him to the barber, you have to make sure his hair is always lined up. Hair is important, especially to our culture."

"Yeah, I know. I figured that out. But his *skin*—I don't think his parents take care of his skin the right way," Frosty said in response.

"Lotion, everything needs lotion," said Elijah. "Hair needs oil. Skin needs lotion. You cannot let it get dry."

"Is there a type of lotion that is best?" Frosty asked.

The conversation continued. The men began to discuss not only Ahmad, but also Paul's and Elijah's families.

My father leans on Paul and Elijah as examples—knowledgeable individuals who have a plethora of information to share. Not only do they educate him on the ins and outs of raising a black boy in America (keeping in mind hair, skin, and playgrounds), but they also open his realities to other parts of life, and vice versa. Paul and Elijah are both role models in my father's life.

During a dinner one evening, when my parents had invited Paul, Elijah, and their families to their house to share a meal, they began talking about racism in the city. As you can tell, this is a common topic when Frosty, Paul, and Elijah get together. They each have something to learn and share.

Paul's young-adult daughter was sitting at the table with the rest of the adults as the conversation turned to different areas around the city. They had all grown up in the city and had seen change over the decades.

Paul said, "Yeah, there are some places I just don't go in the city."

"Why?" Frosty asked.

"Well, I just don't feel comfortable. Like I don't go to the Honda dealership. I do not feel welcome," Paul said.

"Oh, I love it there," commented Frosty. "They are nice and I got to know the manager. They have that great room to sit in while you wait, also."

Silent for just a minute, Paul then said, "They are racist. I don't go there because they are racist, so I bet my experience is different than yours."

Paul's daughter whipped around to face her father "Dad!" his daughter said, astonished and somewhat embarrassed. "You can't say that."

Paul turned to face her and said, "Oh, yeah—no, we can say that here. He understands," Paul said, referring to my father.

"Oh," she said, softly and with some embarrassment.

My father values his friendships with Paul and Elijah, but he is not the only person who has role models in his life. In the last decade, I have learned the importance of role models in my personal life more than ever before. Ms. Reese was a role model when I first had Ahmad; my friends—especially my friends of color—are role models; Jay was a role model; my parents are role models; and my sister is a role model. A role model's skin color does not matter, I have found. What does matter is the life experiences and the willingness to be honest on the topic of race in America. While my role models have come in and out of my life, each one has taught me something new.

One role model that has stayed constant in my life is one of my best friends, Bre. We met in 2011, when I started my doctorate degree; she was a fellow student in the program. She is a biracial female who is strong, opinionated, and understands and appreciates my questions and hardships. She recognizes that people do not place me in the in-group of parents with black children. She accepts that I ask ignorant questions. She knows that Ahmad will need her when he gets older, as will I. She listens to my questions about hair, skin, experiences, and perceptions. She listens, provides answers, and is the person I turn to for help, because I know that I do not know everything. I reach out to her constantly and she is always there with a listening ear and a blunt yet caring response.

While it is important that the people in Ahmad's life have role models to help guide them through life, it is also imperative that Ahmad has role models. His constant male role models have always been my dad and my husband—two white men. Nevertheless, I am very aware that having black male role models is important in his life, although finding them is not always easy. There is only a handful of men Ahmad interacts with who are black: his barber, my father's pastor friends, and his martial arts instructor. I am hoping that as he gets older, he finds role models in the areas of life that he needs.

Physical role models are important, but as a lifelong educator, I also understand the importance of role-model representation in schools, books, movies, television, and media in general. While whiteness is a default in our society for media genres, parents, educators, and media companies have the duty of ensuring that representation is available for all children—not only the white children. Representation must not feed into stereotypes, but instead mirror what children experience in society in all types of situations. However, sometimes guaranteeing that representation will be present in the lives of children is easier said than done, in real life.

While I do not think that it should be hard for media to incorporate diversity and representation, education is a place that is often struck hard with the "default to whiteness." Most teachers are white, female, and Christian. Black males make up only 2 percent of the K-12 school teacher population. Ahmad has never had a male and/or black teacher, even though the majority of students at his school are students of color. When most of the teachers in the American school system are white, questioning and ensuring accurate representation in literature is sometimes put on the back burner. Yet it is imperative that teachers incorporate both heroic and non-heroic people of color into their curriculums in order to provide students of all races with an inclusive education.

Although I believe that the literary representation of black characters defying stereotype threats is important, there is a constant battle within my own family about black representation in books.

"What do you mean, you 'don't think that he should have books about black people'?" I asked, somewhat annoyed. I was talking to my dad in my living room during one of our discussions while I was writing this book.

"I didn't say that. I said that for a while, I was *only* buying him books about black individuals in history and I realized that maybe I was playing into the 'token' black card," my dad said. "He should have books about lots of people; lots of places."

"Oh," I replied. "Well, I think it is important for him to have positive role models. And I think books are one way for him to have them in his life." We were both sitting down, I on the big, gray chair overlooking the front windows and he in the wooden rocking chair I had inherited from his parents.

"I agree, Anni. I just think that sometimes I was unconsciously stereotyping what I was buying him because they were all black biographies," my dad explained. "I realized when I was doing reading buddies at another elementary school in town that the kids did not care if I was black or white. I was there to be someone in their life—a positive influence who spent time with them each week. I think that anyone, no matter their skin color, can be a good influence. I have realized that kids today do not care as much about race as when I was younger. Maybe Ahmad will when he gets older, but right now, I don't see it." He rocked back and forth slowly, causing the chair to creak.

"Okay, I can see that," I said. "I just don't want him to grow up thinking that people with his skin color can't do anything. I guess I am just scared. I don't want him to grow up and think I kept anything from him. I know he is going to want to meet his black family someday and I want him to feel open, free, and able to ask about them, know about them, and meet them. Maybe it is all tangled up in my head," I said.

My father could tell that I was processing Ahmad's future as a socially perceived black man in America—an identity Ahmad does not appear to understand or care about right now.

Role models and representation are important as children grow up. And, in our society, the narrative of present or absent fathers is also something that is referenced often and plagues my thoughts.

When Jay and I began our divorce proceedings, Ahmad was about 9 months old. We were in the thick of arguments, court appearances, and legal battles at the time of Ahmad's first birthday, but regardless of our arguments, we knew that his first birthday was about *him*, and not us. So Jay came. We were cordial. We have pictures together. Jay was the father figure that Ahmad and I needed at the time. However, as is evident in this book, Jay's paternal role did not last long. The man I thought I needed in Ahmad's life soon disappeared, and was replaced with two amazing men that are now Ahmad's father figures: Pop (Dad) and Doug. While they are not black men, they are open to conversations, to receiving guidance, and to the experiences Ahmad seeks out and questions. While representation and role models are important, I have found that, regardless of skin color, a male role model in the life of a boy is important.

12

My Future, His Future, Our Future

*"'I am now convinced more than ever: The crisis of America is the crisis of the black male.' I once wrote those words in a call for fathers of black boys to see the value in being **there** for their offspring. The odds are stacked against this American cohort: disproportionate rates of school failure, unemployment, imprisonment, and death by violence."*

Howell, 2014

"The United States will become a majority-minority in 2044. The minority population is projected to rise to 56 percent of the total in 2060, compared with 38 percent in 2014."

Colby & Ortman, 2015

"Racial oppression starts in our homes, our offices, our cities, and our states, and it can end there as well. So, start talking—not just problems, but solutions. We can do this, together."

Ijeoma Oluo

"What do you think is in store for Ahmad in the future?" I asked Doug one day, as we were scrolling through social media sites on our back porch. It was 2018, and I was in the middle of writing this book. We were sitting next to each other on the loveseat and were decompressing from our days at work and parenting.

"What do you mean?" he asked. I have a tendency to ask open-ended, out-of-the-blue questions, so this was not a shock to him. However, he did want some clarification before answering.

"Like, his future as a black man. Do you think he will be okay?" I asked, still scrolling through my social media pages.

"Yeah. Every time you ask me a question like that it catches me off guard," he laughed.

"What do you mean? When I ask you about his future?" By this point, I had turned to face him.

"No, when you said, 'as a black boy' or 'as a black man,'" he said.

"What?" I asked.

"I often forget that we do not have the same skin color," he explained. "It is easy to forget. Maybe I have normalized it, but it catches me off guard every time you bring it up."

"I think about it all the time."

"I know."

Still facing each other, I said, "But, I kind of know what you mean, I guess. When we first started talking about having kids, I had a hard time processing it because I could not imagine looking down at a baby who was mine and had white skin. In my head, my babies are mixed—even since I was little, I have felt that."

(*Note: Doug and I did not end up having any kids together.*)

While Doug had heard the story of my black baby doll that sings, "I love you. I love you!" when you press her heart, this was the first time I had told him about my trepidations regarding our procreating. Still, he was not surprised.

We live in a country that does not embrace Rev. Martin Luther King Jr.'s *I Have a Dream* speech. People judge other people—their worth, and their capability—on visible differences and descriptors. As we continue to challenge and change mindsets, embracing the words of Dr. King can still be at the heart of our progress. Judge people by the content of their character. Judge people by their actions. Judge people by their invisible capabilities and worth.

No one can predict the future, but my hope is that one day, Ahmad will not be seen as just "a black man in America" who is followed in stores, racially profiled at traffic stops, and discriminated against in the job field. We all still have fears, though. My father's fear is Ahmad growing up, becoming an adolescent, and wondering about the family he doesn't know and the culture that others define him by but that he does not understand.

While my father is not scared for Ahmad to discover more about himself, he is fearful that Ahmad may one day feel rejected or lash out for not being able to experience his biological paternal side of the family.

"What do you think is in store for Ahmad when he gets older?" I asked my dad one sunny afternoon.

"I don't know," he replied. "But I do know that I was hopeful when President Obama was president. But now that Trump is president, everyone has come out of the woodwork. Racism is not gone. With Trump in office, the negative side of America is out—and bolder. That makes me scared for him."

President Obama stated in a 2014 speech that, "We are not a black America, a white America, or a Latino America, but we are the United States of America." In recent years, my response to this has been, "Are we really? Or are we a divided America, growing further and further apart on two sides of spectrum?"

The election of Trump affected my view of the future. With President Trump's rhetoric surrounding a Muslim ban, racist remarks, separating children from their families, and just overall xenophobia, I was (and still am) scared.

The night of the election of President Trump, I was in the middle of a 2.5-hour drive home after teaching a class. I, as well as many other Americans, thought that Hillary Clinton would be elected. I arrived home around 11 p.m. and saw my husband watching the numbers come in. I looked at the television and stopped dead in my tracks. What was I seeing? Trump was going to be our next president. That couldn't be right.

I stayed up a little longer and then finally went to bed, feeling defeated.

The next morning I woke up to the official news: Trump was the new president. I cried—a lot. That day I had to fly to Cleveland, Ohio for a conference. In the airports, the only thing on the television was the analyses of the Trump election. I cried again. But then, in my sorrowful state, I became determined. I got out my computer and logged onto Airbnb. I was taking my son out of this hellhole of a country, at least for the summer. I was no longer sad, but scared and pissed. I was going to protect my son.

I typed in *Toronto, Canada* and looked for places to take Ahmad—places to spend the summer. I called my husband and told him what I was doing.

"Anni. Just take a few days. You are upset right now," he said, from his desk at work.

"Do you know what just happened in our country?" I said angrily.

"Yes," he answered calmly. "I do. But let's just see what happens."

"Fine!" I hung up the phone.

I did not end up moving to Canada with Ahmad for the summer, but that visceral feeling of "get me out of here with my son" will always stay with me.

We are all on our own learning journey in life. It is important for people to ask critical questions that make others reflect. During a sermon my mother gave in a small, rural Illinois church one Sunday, she said, "Do you see lawn jockeys on the front lawns of your neighbors? Do you see the Confederate flag waving in the streets of your town? These are all signs of racism around us." She encouraged the small congregation to stop being complacent and instead to reflect, discuss, and fight to ensure that we are a nation living up to the dream of Dr. Martin Luther King Jr.

Through the evolution of my life— past, present, and future—I remember that we all must continue to fight for justice by breaking down the walls of prejudice. Nothing will change in the future if something is not done in the present. Ignoring race is denying the reality that is staring back at us. There is no such thing as being colorblind to racism. Our institutions and laws, as well as the structure of our country, is built on the back of racism. Striving to erase history by disregarding racism does our country more harm than good. However, when we can begin to understand the impact of our history on lives today, change can happen.

My journey is my journey. I have evolved over my lifetime through experiences, conversations, and reflections, and my evolution continues. I aim to keep an open mind and realize that learning and conversations, specifically about race, can be emotional. But I am willing to take confront emotion in order to advocate for racial justice and equity.

Discomfort around the conversation of race is a huge barrier to any movement toward a more equitable and accepting society. I challenge white parents of children of color to question, learn, and ensure that your child has a diverse community of role models and sees representation through media; I challenge white parents of white children to realize race is also part of your lives and the lives of your children; I challenge parents of color to help other parents who need help navigating our racialized America. I am not asking parents of color to be a spokesperson or to explain everything, but merely to be a person who will not judge a stupid, racist question; a person who has a reciprocal relationship that will be honest and open. A person like Bre. Bre knows I am learning; knows I am growing; and knows that I have done everything in my power to answer a question before reaching out to her. She provides me real-life experiences, honesty, and blunt answers. She will always be in my son's life, as a role model. I am aware of my ignorance and I am cognizant of the fact that I need to find a community of people (or parents) who are willing to help me raise my son to be a strong, confident black man in America.

And while I completely understand how society sees my son, a black man in America, I argue that my son—and every other person—should not be defined by their race. It is not just black and white. It is a fedora-fanatic, bow tie-loving, pink- and blue-outfit-wearing boy (man) making his way through life—who also happens to have brown skin. So, you may see him as a black man in America, and I may need to raise him with the awareness that others view him as a black man in America. But my hope is that one day he will be seen for who is truly is—and not categorized by the box he marks for race.

13

Epilogue

Dear reader, if you have made it to this point in the book, my hope is that you have learned something new, have reflected on something interesting, and have begun or continued the process of growing, learning, and reflecting. My hope is that you have also planned to have or already have engaged in conversations with others about the concept of race—even if it is uncomfortable at times. Painful and distressing emotions lead to growth and learning.

How do *I* continually grow and learn? I make lists: lists of podcasts to listen to, books to read, and articles to include in the courses I teach.

While writing this book in 2018, a friend texted me:

"Do you feel like giving me all the best articles, videos, and podcasts you know of for bias and identity exploration?"

This friend is a fellow educator and is a person of color who is on her own path to discovering how her identity, and the identity of her multiracial child, is seen by the world. She is the woman who many people believed to be Ahmad's mother when we were in public together.

When I got this text message, I was a little overwhelmed. It was a tall order. For the last 10 years (and longer, really) I have been collecting, reading, discovering, discussing, and learning about bias, race, and exploring identity. A few days later, however, I responded positively:

"Oh man, there are so many. But, of course I will. Send me an email so it's on my to-do list."

While the order was tall, I knew that the resource I would create would be a great go-to resource for the readers of this book. It's not an exhaustive list, but it is very personal.

The list provided here is a catalog of articles, podcasts, books, and more. I have collected these resources for the courses I teach or while engaging in my own personal lifelong learning. Please feel free to add your own resources, too, as this is a "living list"—a list that will multiply in size for each person on their own journey.

I do have one request: When you feel yourself pushed past the edge of comfort and into discomfort, keep going. That sweet spot is the place of growth. I have often found myself in that space, of moving from comfort to discomfort. While it may take goal-setting and determination, the progress is worth it. For example, one of the movies listed is *Waiting for "Superman."* In all honesty, I have not yet watched that movie, at the time of writing this book. The premise makes me uncomfortable. I sympathize with the students described in summaries of the movie, and I feel that it would bring back memories of my younger teaching days—in buildings that were falling apart, classrooms that had no heat, and students who were not given the opportunity to achieve their highest potential based purely on the ZIP code they were born into or the education they were provided in schools that sometimes could not provide their most basic needs, shelter and safety. If you have not heard of the movie *Waiting for "Superman,"* the filmmaker follows a handful of promising kids through a system that inhibits, rather than encourages, academic growth. He undertakes and exhaustive review of public education, surveying "dropout factories" and "academic sinkholes." However, the movie embraces the belief that good teachers make good schools—reshaping the school culture refusing to leave students behind.

You are all my accountability partners now, and by the time this book is published, my goal is to leap over my discomfort and watch *Waiting for "Superman."* Therefore, I challenge you to do the same. Maybe not watch that specific movie, but to create a community of accountability partners and strive to leap over the line of comfort and into discomfort. Your eyes will be opened. As you discover your own resources, I ask that you send them to me via the website www.NotJustBlackandWhiteBook.com.

Podcasts

Pod Save The People

Our National Conversation About Conversations About Race

The Stoop

Us and Them

Ear Hustle

Out of the Blocks

Snap Judgment

The Mashup Americans

There Goes the Neighborhood

We Live Here

Yo, Is this Racist?

Code Switch

PostBourgie

Books

So You Want to Talk About Race? by Ijeoma Oluo

Between the World and Me by Ta-Nehisi Coates

The Hate U Give by Angie Thomas

Hillbilly Elegy: A Memoir of a Family and Culture in Crisis by J.D. Vance

Evicted by Matthew Desmond

For White Folks Who Teach in the Hood by Christopher Emdin

Pushout: The Criminalization of Black Girls in Schools by Monique W. Morris

The New Jim Crow by Michelle Alexander

Some of My Best Friends are Black: The Strange Story of Integration in America by Tanner Colby

The Mis-Education of the Negro by Carter G. Woodson

Dear Martin by Nic Stone

Born a Crime by Trevor Noah

Tears We Cannot Stop by Michael Eric Dyson

Why Are All the Black Kids Sitting Together in the Cafeteria?
by Beverly Daniel Tatum

White Trash: The 400-Year Untold History of Class in America by Nancy Isenberg

Courageous Conversations About Race: A Field Guide for Achieving Equity in Schools
by Glenn E. Singleton

Roots by Alex Haley

White Fragility by Robin Diangelo

Funds of Knowledge: Theorizing Practices in Households, Communities, and Classroom
by Norma Gonzalez and Luis C. Moll

*The Trouble with Black Boys: ...And Other Reflections on Race, Equity and the Future
of Public Education* by Pedro A. Noguera

Just Mercy by Bryan Stevenson

Culturally Responsive Teaching and the Brain by Zaretta Hammond

Everyday Anti-Racism by Mica Pollock

The Autobiography of Malcolm X

Articles

*Funds of Knowledge for Teaching: Using a Qualitative Approach to Connect Homes
and Classrooms* (Moll, Amanti, Neff, & Gonzalez)

A Conversation on Race (New York Times) A short film series

21 Racial Microaggressions You Hear on a Daily Basis (BuzzFeed)

Unmasking 'racial microaggressions' (DeAngelis)

White Privilege: Unpacking the Invisible Knapsack (McIntosh)

Cultural Bias in Teaching (Tyler, Stevens, & Ugdh)

Culturally Relevant Pedagogy (Oran)

Recognizing and Addressing Macroaggressions in Teacher-Family Relationships
(Daha)

The Realities of Raising a Kid of a Different Race (Valby)

Music/Artist

This is America (Childish Gambino)
Redemption (Bob Marley)
Buffalo (Bob Marley)
What It Means (Drive-By Truckers)
J. Cole
Solange
Kendrick Lamar
Chance the Rapper

Movies

Get Out
Waiting for "Superman"
Crash
Hidden Figures
Selma
The Color Purple
American History X
Do the Right Thing
To Kill a Mockingbird
Black Panther

In my own growth process, I am seeking a new intergroup/in-group. Throughout my entire life, I have been socially perceived and placed in the in-groups of my outside appearance: white, female, Christian. However, I have more groups to seek—more groups that represent who I am. Finding an in-group that may not be visible to the outside world is difficult, but I am confident it is possible.

So, in your own growth process, talk to others, research, read, and, most importantly, listen with an open mind. America's demographics are changing, and while many individuals push hard against change, demographic change in America is inevitable. Be part of the acceptance and change. Be the change.

Acknowledgment

I would first like to thank my son, Ahmad.

Before writing this book, which primarily focused on his life and the positive impact his life has had on the people around him, I asked his permission. Granting me permission to write about him, Ahmad asking questions during the progress of the story, showing excitement as the book was being completed and motivating me to fully engage and complete the memoir was the encouragement that I needed. This process was not just therapeutic for me; it will be something that he can cherish throughout his life.

I would also like to thank my parents. My dad, Rev. "Frosty" Forrest, has been the rock for our family. He has provided guidance and stability, and is always willing to listen and converse about our family dynamics. Additionally, his sermon and storytelling strategy is echoed in this book. Engaging parishioners through detailed and personal stories has been something I have heard every Sunday morning since I was born. My mom, Rev. "Sue" Susan, has been the wings of our family. She is always reaching out for me and engages in personal and professional growth focused on multicultural topics. My mom has provided me a critical eye with which to view the world—and that was an integral part of the process of writing this memoir.

My husband, Doug, has been my cheerleader, support, stability, and brainstorming partner through this whole process. He has also diligently read and provided feedback multiple times. Beyond supporting me both in this endeavor and professionally, he has provided for Ahmad a stable male figure who is doing his best to raise a caring and confident man.

My family has not been my only support system. My friends and colleagues have also been great supporters during the whole process of motherhood and the writing this memoir. From my experiences with Allison, to my open communication with Bre, to Ahmad's godmother, Heidi (Ms. T)—it truly takes a village. While none of these women live close to me, they are a phone call or a text away. They help me navigate the complexity of race, let me ask questions, and put me in uncomfortable places when needed, in order to grow.

Finally, I would like to thank the individuals and publishing company that guided me through this process. From the initial blind pitch of "Hey, I would like to write a book" email to David Crumm, through phone calls and interactions with other members of his team, I have felt nothing but support and guidance and a focus on my best interests.

To everyone, my roots and my wings: Thank you.

About the Author

Anni K. Reinking, Ed.D., is an assistant professor in the early child-hood program at Southern Illinois University Edwardsville. Professionally, she dedicates her time to research and writing, specifically on the topics of play-based practice, teacher preparation techniques, effective coaching and mentoring strategies, and multicultural education.

This is her first memoir. She felt a calling to write this story as divides within American society continue to widen and her son grows and matures into a socially perceived black man. With the support of her family, colleagues, and friends, Reinking has written several articles, a textbook, and (now) a memoir on race in America, focusing on how it impacts the lives of children and diverse families.

Reinking lives with her husband, son, two stepdaughters, and two cats (Donut and Zoey) in Central Illinois. As a family, they stay busy exploring and finding new adventures—hiking trails, attending music concerts, and visiting as many zoos as possible.

Related Books

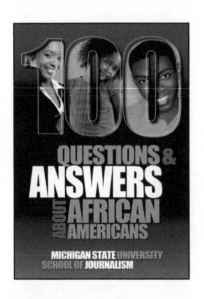

***100 Questions and Answers About
African Americans***

Michigan State University
School of Journalism, 2016

Learn about the racial issues that W.E.B. DuBois
said in 1900 would be the big challenge for the
20th century. This guide explores Black and
African American identity, history, language,
contributions and more. Learn more about
current issues in American cities and campuses.

http://news.jrn.msu.edu/culturalcompetence/

ISBN: 978-1-94201-119-4

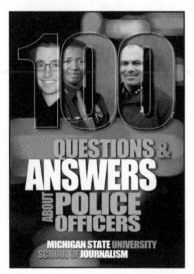

***100 Questions and Answers About
Police Officers***

Michigan State University
School of Journalism, 2018

This simple, introductory guide answers 100 of the
basic questions people ask about police officers,
sheriff's deputies, public safety officers and tribal
police. It focuses on policing at the local level,
where procedures vary from coast to coast. The
guide includes a resource about traffic stops.

http://news.jrn.msu.edu/culturalcompetence/

ISBN: 978-1-64180-013-6

Print and ebooks available on Amazon.com and other retailers.

Related Books

The Black Knight
An African-American Family's Journey from
West Point—a Life of Duty, Honor and Country

by Clifford Worthy

In the 1940s, the U.S. Military Academy at West Point was out of reach for most African Americans due to racial barriers. Clifford Worthy was one of the first who was accepted and excelled as a Black Knight of the Hudson. His courageous Army service around the world balanced military and family life, even as they raised a child with special needs.

TheBlackKnightBook.com

ISBN: 978-1-64180-030-3

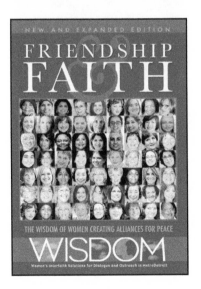

Friendship and Faith
The WISDOM of women creating
alliances for peace

The Women of WISDOM

This is a book about making friends, which may be the most important thing you can do to make the world a better place, and transform your own life in the process. Making a new friend often is tricky, as you'll discover in these dozens of real-life stories by women from a wide variety of religious and ethnic backgrounds. But, crossing lines of religion, race and culture is worth the effort, often forming some of life's deepest friendships, these women have found. In *Friendship and Faith*, you'll discover how we really can change the world one friend at a time.

InterfaithWisdom.com

ISBN: 978-1-94201-193-4

Print and ebooks available on Amazon.com and other retailers.

CPSIA information can be obtained
at www.ICGtesting.com
Printed in the USA
FFHW020655181218
49915023-54526FF